FORSAKEN

FORSAKEN

The Persecution of Christians
in Today's Middle East

DANIEL WILLIAMS

OR Books
New York · London

Published by OR Books, New York and London
Visit our website at **www.orbooks.com**

First printing 2016

Cataloging-in-Publication data is available from the Library of Congress. A catalog record for this book is available from the British Library.

ISBN 978-1-68219-034-0 paperback
ISBN 978-1-68219-035-7 e-book

This book is set in Amalia. Typeset by AarkMany Media, Chennai, India. Printed by BookMobile in the US and CPI Books Ltd in the UK.

TABLE OF CONTENTS

1/ INTRODUCTION TO A LOST CAUSE

My God, my God, why hast Thou forsaken me?

—Matthew 27:46

In the homeland of Christianity, war, intolerance, and political maneuvering are obliterating the Christian population. Killings and mass expulsion are the trademarks of the severest repression. Community after community is resorting to emigration to survive.

For Christians, the Holy Land means more than the Palestine where Jesus walked. It includes the places where the first Christian communities and churches sprang up, from present-day, war-torn Iraq and Syria across to tumultuous Egypt.

The territory is now an incubator both for anti-Christian violence and generalized terrorism across the globe. Christians are victims of expanded interpretations of jihad, the Islamic tradition of holy war. On the basis of these doctrines, radical armed groups like al-Qaeda and the Islamic State of Iraq and Sham (ISIS) justify murder, looting, and full-scale expulsions of civilians. (Sham is an Arabic term for Greater Syria, which once stretched from the border of Turkey through Palestine.) Beyond the Holy Land, copycat murderous campaigns have spread to countries as far afield as Kenya, Nigeria, Libya, and France.

Christian migration has been going on for centuries, due to economic hardship, chronic conflict, and the difficulties of living as a minority. Now, state collapse, radical sectarian insurgency, and persistent political repression have turned migration into mass flight and collective extinction.

The impact on Christians is dramatic. Twelve years after a US-led invasion upended the dictatorship of Saddam Hussein, Iraq's Christian population has shrunk from well over one million to 300,000, maybe less—and even this remnant is flooding into exile. In June 2014, extremists of the Islamic State took over Mosul, Iraq's second largest city. The terrorist group presented the city's remaining 30,000 Christian residents with a choice: either convert to Islam, pay protection money, leave, or die. The entire Christian population fled within days.

In the chaos, the invaders confiscated homes and businesses, abducted women into slavery, and held children for ransom. They stripped the elderly and the sick of their few valuables (women's gold matrimonial earrings were attractive loot) and then forced them to walk miles under the hot sun to escape.

Syria is where the word "Christian" was first coined, some two thousand years ago. At least 500,000 Syrian Christians out of a total population of 1.5 million have fled their homes during almost five years of civil war. Muslim insurgents fighting the government of Bashar al-Assad have publicly executed Christians, kidnapped others, and sacked churches and schools. As in Iraq, convert-or-die threats have been common. The sectarian fury of the rebellion has compelled Christians into the hands of the cruel Assad regime.

The Christian dilemma extends beyond these two countries at war. In Egypt, whose Coptic church is co-equal in age with the Church of Rome and Eastern Churches, political turmoil has unleashed outrage and attacks against the Christian community. Numbering between five and seven million believers, the Coptic Church is the Middle East's largest single Christian sect. Copts are now migrating to the US, Canada, and Australia. Those who remain are resented by Egyptians who blame them for the 2013 military ouster of elected Muslim president Mohammed Morsi and the birth of a new dictatorship.

In chronically restive Lebanon and the Palestinian Territories, Christian communities are confronted by economic hardship, periodic warfare, creeping ascendancy of political Islam and radical jihad. Fifty years ago, half Lebanon's population was Christian. It is now down to 35 per cent. Fifty years ago, 10 per cent of Palestinians in the West Bank and Gaza Strip were Christians. The ratio is now 2 per cent—about 73,000 people—with the relative decline due to emigration as well as high Muslim birth rates. The dwindling numbers have been accompanied by a palpable sense of social and political marginalization.

Only in Israel is the Christian population, about 163,000, on the increase. Though spared the harsh military occupation imposed on Palestinians in the occupied territories, and despite residing under a relatively liberal legal regime, Christians in Israel live in an uneasy limbo. They are caught between sympathy for Palestinian independence and Israel's efforts to exploit sectarian tensions and lure them from identification with the Palestinian cause.

As the vicious civil wars in Iraq and Syria demonstrate, persecution of Christians is also part of a wider maelstrom of violence in the Holy Land largely between Sunni Islam and Shiite Islam. Sunni jihadists in particular conflate Christians with their Shiite enemies, declaring open season on Christians in both Iraq and Syria. Intolerant Sunni Islam sects contribute to Christian insecurity beyond the countries at war.

The fate of Christians in the Holy Land should create special alarm outside the region—much as a deep look at the circumstances of Jews in 1930s Germany or the tribal bigotry in 1990s Rwanda ought to have warned then of ravages to come.

Worldwide expressions of unease are many, but actions few. On April 12, 2015, Pope Francis voiced concern at the world's complacency over attacks on Christians, and spoke of a looming "third world war" of religious conflict.

He continued: "All who are Heads of State and of International Organizations are called to oppose such crimes with a firm sense of duty, without ceding to ambiguity or compromise."

Muslims are far from immune. In late 2014, when I was speaking with Christian refugees in Kurdistan, a photograph and message arrived on the mobile phone of one of the men I was interviewing. It was from Mosul and the photo showed a Muslim friend of his whose back was crisscrossed with whip marks. He had been punished by the Islamic State for critical remarks he published on Facebook. Another acquaintance sent an email explaining how he was threatened with beheading because he tried to prevent confiscation of a Christian-owned furniture store.

The ideological source of such threats is no secret. They originate in ultra-conservative Salafi and Wahhabi movements within Islam, for whom Christians are, at best, dispensable. Hardline followers are active not only in war-ravaged Iraq and Syria, but also Egypt, Lebanon, Palestine, and Israel.

While persecution escalates, critics and defenders of Islam have entered into a sterile debate about whether anti-Christian violence has everything or nothing to do with Islam. Both are misguided.

Critics must recognize that during Islamic history, treatment of minorities has varied and many examples of tolerance thrive within the world of Islam.

Defenders, on the other hand, ought to stop pretending that jihadist violence is divorced from many texts and practices of Islam through the centuries. The jihadists' justifications may be cherry-picked and their conclusions faulty, but they do not resort to falsification: their written sources and historical precedents are authentic.

This is not the first time in Islamic history that the framework of jihad has included repression directed against Christians. On occasion, it occurred on the whims of a ruler. Mostly, however, attacks on Christianity, along with emphasis on assaulting non-combatant Christian communities, emerged when Islam felt itself under threat from outside powers.

The Crusades, when European Christian invaders undermined Islam's hold on the Holy Land, were one example. Christians also became targets of violence as the Ottoman Empire crumbled and then later, in the late nineteenth and first half of the twentieth century, during colonial control of the region.

In recent decades, a string of perceived debacles fueled the appeal of jihad: the establishment of the State of Israel, the Arab defeats in the 1948 and 1967 Middle East Wars, subsequent chronic hostilities between Israel and the Palestinians as well as Lebanon, and—perhaps most relevant to the current upheavals—the US-led 2003 invasion of Iraq, launched to remake the Middle East in a made-in-Washington Western image.

The West seems unwilling to speak out clearly against Christian persecution. Indeed, Western leaders often refuse to acknowledge that past colonial policies and recent wars have anything to do with the recent turmoil. The French and British in particular played on, and nurtured, sectarian differences as a strategy to weaken Arab nationalism during their post-World War II domination of the region.

Many leaders in the West fail to acknowledge that their promiscuous use of force created conditions that jihadists could exploit to justify their extreme actions, including the persecution of Christian communities.

During the US occupation of Iraq, the Bush government declined to provide for special protection of Christians for fear that to officially define Iraqi turmoil as sectarian would somehow intensify the rivalries. And yet it was the US-led war that opened the way to Iraq's division into warring ethnic and religious groups.

This turbulent context ought not be used to obscure the glaring fact that Christians are being targeted simply because they are Christians. Even outside the war zones of Iraq and Syria, political trends suggest that co-existence between Christians and Muslims is reaching an end.

The stakes are high. Everyone should recognize that persecution of Christians is a herald of terror tactics that spill beyond the region. Westerners should acknowledge that both long-past and recent meddling has engendered some of the sectarian hatred they now deplore. Muslims should recognize that, even if not a single Christian remained in the Holy Land, Muslim-on-Muslim warfare will continue and relentless terror endure, all to Islam's detriment.

To people outside the region, Christian communities in the Holy Land are exotic. They have odd, indecipherable names. Their theological differences with mainstream Catholic and Western Protestant sects are obscure. Yet, these churches were the original heart of a religion that spread throughout much of the world.

The decline of these Christian populations, whether Orthodox, Catholic or part of the Eastern Church community or Protestant, is not only a human tragedy but an historic cataclysm. An integral part of the region's fabric is being ripped away. The marks of Christian contributions to Middle East civilization are everywhere. They built cities, framed politics, shaped values, fought colonial adventurers, and bridged the East–West divide.

Christians played a prominent role in the late nineteenth and early twentieth century cultural renewal known as the Arab Renaissance. A Christian, Butros al-Bustani, translated the Bible into Arabic and penned the first Arab-language encyclopedia. Nassif Yazigi, a Greek Catholic, promoted the revival of classical Arabic literature. Jurji Zaydan, a Greek Orthodox, wrote novels popularizing Arab history. These luminaries believed themselves to be contributors to a civilization of which they were a vital part.

The Christian saga began two thousand years ago when a Jewish traveler named Paul, fresh from a trip to Jerusalem, was suddenly stricken blind on the road to Damascus. In Jerusalem, he had been engaged in persecuting followers of a Jewish preacher named Jesus. When he got to Damascus, he took refuge on a street called Straight. Three days later a man from the neighborhood came and cured him, on orders from God. Paul became a follower of Christ.

He was the first to distinguish Jesus' followers from Jews. He preached throughout Syria and along Mediterranean shores. Other Christian pioneers—apostles and disciples—spread the new belief into Egypt and Mesopotamia.

These early churches may seem insignificant to ethnocentric Westerners, but they sowed the seeds of global Christian culture. Antioch, now Antakya in Turkey, and Alexandria in Egypt, were, along with Rome, the first main apostolic "Holy Sees" of

Christianity. The churches in Mesopotamia—present-day Iraq—spread their message into India and to distant China.

From the beginning, the Holy Land was a tempestuous neighborhood and Christians suffered from chronic regional conflict. The area is the original battleground of the age-old East–West struggle. Alexander the Great took on the Persians. Rome conquered Syria and Palestine and then Rome's heir, the Byzantine Empire, faced off against Persia. Islamic Arab armies conquered Persia, devoured much of the Byzantine Empire and moved into Europe by force of arms.

The transition from pagan Rome to Byzantium's official Christianity delivered no concord among the faithful. Christians squabbled among themselves over minute details of theology. The imperial church in Constantinople tried to impose unity, but localized churches sometimes refused to go along.

The Byzantine Empire was progressively enfeebled by constant war with Persia. In the seventh century, armies fighting under the banner of a new monotheistic religion emerged from Arabia. Exhausted Byzantium retreated.

Christian theological disputes played a role in Islam's conquest of the Holy Land. Some Christians welcomed the invaders: the conquering religion preached a faith not bound up in debates over Trinity and the nature of Christ and required no more than an expression of faith to join.

Arab Muslims came into possession of an archipelago of functioning, even rich, societies. The Fertile Crescent that spans the Holy Land was not only bountiful but also a major trade route that linked three continents. There were magnificent cities—Damascus, Alexandria, and Antioch among them—as well as the fortress town of Jerusalem, dear to both Christians and Jews.

Christians were the majority population. The new rulers decided the exercise of soft power, rather than violent oppression, was the best policy.

A model in this respect was the subjugation and administration of Jerusalem by the Muslims. In 637 AD, Omar Ibn Khattab conquered the city after a long siege. Sophronius, the Byzantine patriarch of the city, decided that surrender was the better part of valor. Terms were relatively generous: Byzantine-armed loyalists could leave peacefully and Christian residents could stay so long as they paid a poll tax to the conquerors. No churches, homes, or businesses would be destroyed and religious life could continue as before.

Omar toured the city and visited the ancient site of the razed Jewish Temple, where he ordered construction of a mosque. He declined Sophronius' invitation to enter the Church of the Holy Sepulcher on the grounds that, once he went in, his followers would convert the building into a mosque.

His refusal to enter the church set the mythical basis of the status quo that supposedly guides religious sites in Jerusalem's Old City up to today (but which is threatened by fundamentalist Jewish efforts to place a new Jewish Temple on the grounds of Omar's al-Aqsa Mosque complex). Similar scenes of surrender were played out across the region. Muslim invaders combined force with deft negotiation to subdue a land left adrift.

Nonetheless, Islam's assertion of superiority was integral to Muslim rule and an enduring source of Christian insecurity. When Omar's succesors decorated the octagonal Dome of the Rock on the old Temple site, they included Koranic verses puncturing Christian dogma. The magnificence of the Dome was meant to outshine the Holy Sepulcher church just down the street. In the ninth century, various versions of surrender documents known as the "Pact of Omar" (not to be confused with Omar's treaty with Sophronius in Jerusalem) set numerous restrictions on Christians living under Islam, including prohibitions on building new, or repairing old, churches.

From the seventh century on, except during periods of the Medieval Crusades, all Christians in the Greater Holy Land lived under Muslim rule. Early Islamic civilization incorporated the many cultures under Arab control in a spirit of relative tolerance. Christian scholars translated Greek and Latin philosophical texts. Christian merchants frequently thrived. Christians served in high positions in Islamic government and many followers of Christ also converted.

But Christian well-being often depended on the politics of the moment and the moods of Muslim caliphs, sultans, and local governors.

Christian vulnerability was rarely more evident than during the early eleventh-century reign of Hakim bi-Amr Allah, the Shiite Fatimid caliph in Cairo. The 260 years of Shiite rule across the Holy Land were mostly devoid of threats to Christians, but Hakim went on a rampage, destroying churches in Egypt, Syria, and Palestine, including the Church of the Holy Sepulcher. He forced Christians (and Jews) to wear heavy necklaces—in the case of Christians, made of iron; uncomfortable gear that distinguished Christians as inferior. The restrictions were lifted by his successors and the repression faded.

During the Crusades, guilt-by-religious association inspired attacks on Christians by Muslim attacks on Christians. It made no difference that the invading Roman Catholic Crusaders held many indigenous Christians in contempt due to old theological disagreements. The more menace from outside that was felt by the Islamic empire, the more Muslims focused hostility on Christians within.

This was especially so during the thirteenth century, when Crusaders and Mongols launched contemporaneous assaults on the empire of the Cairo-based Mamelukes. Mamelukes were a slave class that had newly conquered the empire of their masters. They promoted schools of Sunni Islamic thought and jurisprudence that were hostile to Christians. During the Seventh Crusade, some Christian communities supported the invaders and allied themselves with established Crusader states in the Levant. In the east, Assyrian Christians welcomed the Mongols, who seemed tolerant of religious belief so long as conquered subjects were loyal. (Disloyal subjects, on the other hand, were treated with unsparing viciousness: when the Mongols under Genghis Khan conquered and razed Baghdad, the Tigris and Euphrates rivers famously ran with blood.)

The Mamelukes drove out both the Crusaders and Mongols from the Holy Land and perpetual suspicion of indigenous Christians became a guiding force of jihad. Christians became a minority in the region as onerous taxes and repression impelled many to convert to Islam.

European colonialism revived ancient anti-Christian feelings. Napoleon invaded Egypt in 1798 but was driven out. The British attacked Egypt in 1882 over debt payments and stayed until the 1950s. Colonialists also presented themselves as defenders of minorities, in particular Christians, to justify their rule. Islamic politics consciously developed as a response to foreign intrusion and Muslim suspicions of indigenous Christians grew.

From the fifteenth to the twentieth century, during the era of Ottoman imperial rule, formal Christian inferiority occasionally went hand in hand with service in the sovereign bureaucracy. Christians comprised the bulk of the sultan's private army—on condition that they not marry.

As the Ottoman Empire crumbled in the early twentieth century, conditions for Christians dramatically worsened. The Turkish Ottomans suspected Christian Armenians of betrayal in the service of their enemies, especially Russia. The Turks slaughtered tens of thousands in what has become known as the Armenian Holocaust.

Whether the massacre of Armenian Christians resulted from a notion of holy war has long been a subject of debate— Ottoman and Turkish reformers in the early twentieth century were nominally atheist. Clearly, however, Islam's designation of Christians as inferior lingered both during the reform period and the fall of the empire and underpinned the violence. Imams and Islamic scholars railed against any Ottoman political change that suggested equality among all religious faiths.

In the twentieth century, Christian activists in the Holy Land made efforts to end their second-class status through political involvement. They did so by presenting themselves as nationalists first rather than Christians.

A Christian, Michel Aflaq, developed Baathism, the pan-Arab secular ideology that was the nominal basis for the rule of Iraq's Saddam Hussein and Syria's Bashar al-Assad. Socialism, as a class-based framework for overriding sectarian differences, attracted other Christian activists. Still others enthusiastically participated in anti-colonial movements even as European overlords tried to seduce them with favors.

Following the Arab defeat in the 1967 war with Israel, Islamic political movements burgeoned. Adherents believed that the cure for Arab weakness lay in the imposition of strict religious norms on society. They began to label indigenous Christians, not to mention followers of European and American Protestantism, as Fifth Columnists.

The 2003 conquest of Iraq by US-led forces marked a tipping point. The war unleashed movements that branded Christians allies of the foreign enemy and unworthy of living under Islam. Sunni rebels also conflated Christians with the Shiite-dominated government that the invaders installed in Baghdad.

In Iraq, al-Qaeda and the Islamic State both regarded Christianity as anathema. Each also took part in the Syrian rebellion against the Assad regime; Christians there, too, became a target.

Meanwhile, Salafis and their Muslim followers assaulted Christians and churches in Egypt. In the Palestinian Territories, Islamic formulas for ending the Israeli occupation of the West

Bank and Gaza gradually marginalized Christians from taking part in the national movement.

Only in Lebanon was a kind of shaky status quo reached, and only after much bloodshed. Beginning in 1975, Christians tried to expand their already formidable grip on Lebanese politics. In 1989, after a fifteen-year civil war, Christian political power was weakened through a revamped power-sharing agreement. Sunni–Shiite rivalry became the focus of conflict in Lebanon.

Throughout the Holy Land, what had begun in the seventh century as an imperial experiment in multicultural coexistence degenerated over time into a pit of intolerance and, for Christian communities, gradual extinction.

For Western and Muslim political leaders alike, today's violence against Christians, and any minority in the Holy Land, ought to trigger the application of international law. Systematic attacks on peaceful communities, be they Christian, Sunni or Shiite Muslim, or other religious and ethnic groups, are prohibited in wartime and as well as within societies not at war. Perpetrators of attacks on civilians should be charged with war crimes or crimes against humanity.

The situation of Christians in Iraq and Syria requires urgent action. That means, at minimum, the provision of adequate refuge and protection for Christians and others displaced by war.

All this is doable. But the painful truth is that for the foreseeable future, by virtue of a declining population and resurgent Islamist politics, the Holy Land is fast becoming a museum of a lost culture.

2/ THE HOLY WAR ON CHRISTIANS

Kill the idolaters wherever you find them, take them, besiege them, and lie in wait for them at every point of observation. If they repent afterwards, perform the prayer and pay the alms, then release them.

Allah is truly all-forgiving, merciful.

—Koran 9:5, the "Verse of the Sword"

In late December 2014, twenty-one Coptic Christians from Egypt and one companion from Chad, all migrant workers, were captured in Libya by members of a local offshoot of the Islamic State, the militia and terror group that had taken over parts of Iraq and Syria.

A month later, the kidnappers beheaded the captives on video. As they forced the men to their knees, the killers accused the victims of belonging to the hostile "Crusader" Coptic Church of Egypt. Presumably this was meant to link the victims, and all Copts, to the West, which is the prime Islamic State enemy. The declaration also associated them with an event that, in the eyes of not a few Muslims, represents eternal Christian hostility toward Islam.

But the Crusader reference was inappropriate. The Coptic Church is a two-thousand-year-old indigenous Egyptian religion that neither initiated nor participated in the Crusades. The Crusades were launched from Europe by the Roman Catholic Church at a time when Rome was also hostile to the Copts. But such is the nature of the contemporary radical Islam in the Middle East that all Christians are viewed through the distorted lens of religious and historical misconceptions.

Justification for persecuting Christians is based on the latest revision of jihad, the theory and practice of Islamic holy war. To understand the horrendous killings, looting, and expulsions of Christian communities, it is necessary to comprehend contemporary jihad's ideological roots. To fight them,it is necessary to realize that alternatives to their ideas exist within Islam.

Critics of Islam regard the cruelties of radical jihad as typical of the entire religion. This is not so and such commentaries are best seen as an attempt evade discussion and acknowledgement of Western responsibility for Holy Land violence. These critics also ignore that fact that, over the centuries, Muslims have set rules of engagement aimed at regulating warfare. Many of these are similar to limits that evolved in the West.

Defenders of Islam suffer from a different myopia, that is also useful in evading responsibility. They contend that contemporary jihad has nothing to do with the Islamic religion. This is inaccurate. The "Verse of the Sword," cited above, with its a Koranic injunctions against "idolaters," is a favorite among contemporary jihadists. It is not something pulled out of thin air and jihadists cite plenty of well-known Islamic scholars and jurists to justify their tactics.

Responding to jihadist violence with defensive boilerplate—"This is not Islam"—overshadows the fact that many scholars and religious leaders are able to challenge the jihadists' interpretation of Muslim doctrine point by point and have done so. Backing these moderate opinions would require a very public ideological battle that many Islamic leaders prefer to avoid for the sake of a storybook Islamic unity. But the battle is a necessary one, in order to discredit ideas that sanction persecution of Christians, other minorities, and Muslims as well.

Jihad has many meanings. The word literally signifies "striving" or "struggle," though since the dawn of Islam its primary focus was the need to do battle "in God's path," against Islam's early enemies in the Arabian Peninsula and beyond.

Jihad was enjoined in both the Koran and in the hadith, a collection of accepted sayings and acts of Muhammad. Jihad is not a basic pillar of belief (as are: the declaration that only one God exists, pilgrimage to Mecca, giving to the poor, fasting during the holy month of Ramadan, and prayer five times a day).

It is nonetheless an authentic feature of Islam. Current terrorist groups have virtually raised jihad to the level of a sixth pillar.

Over the centuries, Islamic scholars, jurists, and military men molded jihad theory to meet the circumstances of their time. Such is the flexibility of Islam. Sometimes aggressive conquest was foremost, as in the early years. Other times, defense of Islam and its territories were the focus, as when conquests stalled. On other occasions, jihad was simply defined as a call for Muslims to put their spiritual house in order, though that has been at most a secondary purpose.

Tension between jihad and the requirements of governing non-Muslims emerged quickly after the conquest of the Holy Land by Islamic Arab armies. When these forces burst from Arabia, the idea of killing or expelling all Christians was neither contemplated nor considered desirable. Christians were, after all, the majority population in functioning societies. The Arabs were taking over empires, not destroying them.

In the eighth century, Islamic expansion stalled at Spain's frontiers with France and at the limits of Persian and Byzantine territory in the east. The new rulers set aside jihad as a framework for conquest and focused on running an empire with a large non-Muslim population.

Christians in these lands were tolerated provided they paid a tax known as jizya. Some converted and brought their native notions of government and values into Islam. Others, retaining their faith, nonetheless served in Islamic courts and bureaucracy. Early Islam was an era of curiosity. Intellectual and scientific texts, as well as literature from conquered Christian and Persian lands and beyond, were translated into the new lingua franca: Arabic.

Invasion by outside Christian forces did not necessarily taint indigenous Christians. Early in the twelfth century, after the First Crusade had gone badly for the Muslims, appeals for revival of jihad were commonplace. Papal armies had established a kingdom along the Mediterranean coast, which included Jerusalem, already enshrined as an Islamic holy city. Meanwhile, in Sicily and Spain, Christian insurgents conquered territory that had been under Islamic rule for centuries.

To reverse this trend, a Sunni preacher in Damascus, Ali ibn Tahir al-Sulami, exhorted Muslims to take up defense as a religious duty. Speaking at the Great Mosque in Damascus in 1105, al-Sulami crystallized jihad theory and laid out a basic handbook for action over centuries to come.

He insisted that jihad was a duty, "incumbent on all who are capable and have no horrible illness or chronic malady, or blindness, or weakness from old age." He chastised Muslim leaders for ignoring jihad and suggested that everyone practice a "greater" jihad, the cleaning up of one's own religious act. He also called on Sunnis, members of the dominant orthodox sect in the east, to defeat Shiite Muslims, who ruled western regions centered on Egypt. Although Sulami primarily promoted jihad as a defensive duty, he spoke invitingly of a future conquest of Constantinople, the capital of the Byzantine Empire and a powerful bulwark of Christendom.

Al-Sulami did not include persecution of Holy Land Christians among his prescriptions. He referred to the outside invaders as Franks, not Christians.

Nonetheless, the idea that native Christians might collaborate with foreign attackers was never far from the surface—especially during later Islamic dynasties.

In the twelfth and thirteenth centuries, Christian co-operation with invaders of the Seventh Crusade and with Mongol armies that exploded into the Holy Land from Asia deepened such suspicions. The invasions challenged the dearly held assertion that Islam was invincible. Revising jihad became a hot topic among the Mameluke rulers of the time.

The scholar Ibn Taymiyyah justified jihad fully in religious terms—adherence to the Koran and the sword became co-equal as vehicles to sustain the religion. Anyone who stands in the way "must be fought." Obstacles to Islam's triumph included not only the presence of infidels but of timid Muslims and their leaders. Ibn Taymiyyah's writings are basic to current theories of jihad.

Debates over jihad included questions of how to treat civilians, women, children, and prisoners, as well as restrictions on the use of fire, the medieval weapon of mass destruction. In the fourteenth century, the Egyptian scholar Ibn Naqib al-Masri set limits on the destruction of property and forbade killing women and children (though the women could be enslaved). He also raised the possibility that prisoners of war could simply be released if in the "interests" of Islam.

Fast forward to the twenty-first century. The fundamentals of jihad theory remain, to a significant extent, unchanged. Exponents still pledge to unite Muslims and battle an external threat—now "Crusaders and Jews." War on "polytheists" remains paramount, targeting not only Christians but other minorities including the Shiite rulers in Iran and Iraq, and the Alawites, a Shiite offshoot that dominates the government of Syria.

Contemporary jihadists still rail against Muslim leaders who shun jihad. Dying in battle is, now as then, considered a virtue to be rewarded in heaven. Conquest remains a goal, including the eventual taking of Rome and Spain.

But fresh twists have been added. The jihadists expanded martyrdom to include suicide missions; suicide is traditionally forbidden under Islam, but has been redefined as self-sacrifice in the name of jihad. Murderous assaults on innocent civilians, also formerly circumscribed, are permissible. Anyone perceived to support an invader is deemed a combatant, even if their only sin is to vote or pay taxes to an enemy government. Helpless prisoners are regularly and summarily executed.

Human rights and limits as enshrined in the Geneva Convention are considered alien inventions. Not only do the jihadists criticize Muslim leaders who are unwilling to defend Islam, they declare them apostate and therefore targets for death.

Contemporary jihadists contend that Muslims ought to flaunt the superiority of their religion. That means unrelenting humiliation of perceived inferiors. Christians must live under strict Muslim social rules; outward signs of Christianity are to be erased and public festivities canceled. Alcohol shops must close. Women must be covered up in public and girls and boys educated separately. Property is subject to confiscation and children and women consigned to slavery. The jihadists sanction beheadings and crucifixions and forced expulsions under the gun.

These strictures are rooted in Salafism and Wahhabism, two ultra-conservative and intolerant branches of Sunni Islam. Salafism, from the Arabic salaf al-salih, meaning the "righteous predecessors," developed from the ninth century onward. The sect contends that the only model for authentic Muslim life is the word and the practice of the Prophet Mohammed and his earliest associates. The Koran is the sole and supreme source of moral judgement; the individual has no responsibility to discern right from wrong, only to faithfully obey. Influences that informed later Islamic governments are invalid.

For Salafis, life is full of restrictions: on dress and diet, on relations with women, on women themselves. Friendly relations with errant Muslims, not to mention non-Muslims, are forbidden. Once, an Islamic scholar in Egypt raised an outcry when he suggested that for men to be in the same office with a woman, she had to breast-feed them, so to create a maternal rather than potentially sexual, bond.

Wahhabis shares much of the ultra-conservative outlook of Salafis, but developed later and independently. The sect is named for eighteenth-century Islamic ideologue Muhammad ibn Abdul Wahhab who preached a revivalist Islam in a remote area of Saudi Arabia.

Wahhab promoted Islamic purity unsullied by outside influences and pronounced various unauthorized practices as "nullifying" true Islam. For Wahhab, Muslims who avoided jihad were effectively heretics.

In the middle of the eighteenth century, Wahhab contracted an alliance with a local Arab leader. In return for Wahhabi loyalty, the tribal leader, Muhammad ibn Saud, would protect and propagate Wahhabism. Saud and his descendants conquered much of the Arabian Peninsula, and spread Wahhabi teaching across the desert expanse. The family rules Saudi Arabia today and has used the country's oil wealth to extend the Wahhabi message across the Islamic world via television and support for mosques and education.

These ultra-conservatives deny and repudiate sources of Muslim culture and authority and a dynamic engagement with diverse nations and faiths that gave birth to Islamic civilization. Salafis and Wahhabis imagine an Islam born in pristine isolation. They pretend that the early Muslims had no contact with traders and no communication with members of surrounding cultures, except to compel surrender. For them, the tolerance and vibrant cultural intercourse of the Golden Age of Islamic rule in tenth- and eleventh-century Spain never happened. When Osama bin Laden spoke of conquering Andalusia, he did not have in mind a society where Greek and Latin texts on philosophy and science were eagerly translated into Arabic.

Salafis and Wahhabis consider the very presence of Christians as an affront. In their view, Christians have brought Islam to its knees. They sully Islam to the point that even the sight of crosses on churches is an offense. The ultra-conservatives base prohibitions on Christians on the "Pact of Omar," treaties supposedly worked out between Islamic conquerors and Christians who surrendered to Arab armies in Syria.

Christian persecution can't be separated from hostile Salafi and Wahhabi attitudes toward other Muslims. Early targets of

Wahhabis included Sufis, from a branch of Sunni Islam, and Shiites, both of whose practices offended Wahhabi purism. In 1802,
Wahhabi marauders from Arabia attacked Karbala in present-day
Iraq, a city cherished by Shiites because the tomb of Hussein, a
martyred Shiite imam, is located there. Reverence for holy men
is condemned by Salafis and Wahhabis; the Wahhabis burned the
shrine and sacked the city.

Salafis and Wahhabis also disdain smaller Shiite offshoots—
Ismailis, Druze, and Alawites—and of course, Jews. Followers of
religions not drawn from the monotheistic tradition of the Holy
Land are totally out of bounds.

Present-day jihadists feast on ideas that were expounded
during the darkest days of Islam, when both Mongols and
Crusaders encroached on Muslim-ruled land. They ignore texts
and precedents that embrace tolerance and shove aside the
Koran's pronouncement that religion cannot be coerced.

They ignore prohibitions on atrocities put forward by scholars, even those who are otherwise known for promoting jihad.
The Andalusian sage Ibn Hazm was a fierce critic of Christian and
Jewish theology, yet in terms of warfare, he counseled against the
slaying of women. He endorsed the killing of any male during
wartime, but left the ultimate decision to combatants.

Another Andalusian scholar, Ibn al-Arabi, said that Muslims in battle could kill only actual combatants. Neo-jihadists, a

minority among Muslims, ignore all that. They embrace acts that were once forbidden, including terror against civilians and suicide assaults.

Mainstream Muslim scholars and, in my experience, the Muslim population at large do not subscribe to ultra-conservative and exclusionary Islamic theories. But a small number of people can make a huge impact. In historical accounts, jihad conjures up the image of multitudes on horseback fighting armored knights on the plains of Palestine; today's jihad can consist of a single person dropping a homemade bomb in a garbage can in front of a church. And the message can be spread worldwide by the Internet.

The cause of the jihadist ascendance—into something often called "radical jihad" in the West—is the subject of much commentary from both Western and Islamic observers. Its rise is often viewed as a response to the chronic woes and turmoil of Muslim-majority countries in the Holy Land: the Arab military disaster of the 1967 war with Israel, the subsequent inability to resolve the Palestinian–Israeli conflict, periodic Israeli assaults on Gaza and Sunni-dominated Beirut, corruption and cruelty of secular Arab governments, the unending poverty of the masses of Arab people, and the unthinking military and political interventions in the Middle East by Western powers, in particular the United States.

Wahhabis and Salafis preach a mythically untainted Islam as a cure-all. Persecution of Christians is among their remedies for strengthening the Islamic world.

In the 1950s, Sayyid Qutb, a member of Egypt's Muslim Brotherhood, was among the most influential proponents of these Islamic fixes. He rejected all things Western and described Western life as irretrievably degenerate. Muslim societies, he said, were trapped in a polluted world he labeled jahiliyyah— ignorance of God's guidance.

Qutb's view of Christians was in some respects traditional. Under Islam, they would be permitted to practice their religion, but subject to tight restrictions: they must worship in private and their churches must have no outward indicators of faith, including crosses and the sound of bells. These, he thought, might jeopardize Islam's hold on Muslims.

Al-Qaeda, the terror group founded by Osama bin Laden, tightened Qutb's restraints. Al-Qaeda writer Ali al-Aliyani accepted the idea of tolerance only so long as it was "clothed in humiliation and submissiveness." Degenerate Christian practices must be kept away from Muslims. He insisted on "the subjection of the people paying the *jizya* to the laws of Islam, together with forbidding them from openly proclaiming their religions and forbidding them from involving themselves with interest (on loans), fornication, or other things. . . ."

Al-Aliyani expressed no ambiguity about the eventual solution: "O Allah, destroy the Jews, the Christians, and the polytheists, and whoever has befriended them or helped them in any way against your servants the believers."

In 2007, the Islamic State in Iraq, forerunner of ISIS, issued a series of ideological guidelines for jihad. Among them was an unprecedented cancellation of traditional Islamic tolerance for Christians (as well as the other "People of the Book," the Jews):

"We believe that the factions of the People of the Book, and those of their ilk such as the Sabeans [a small Gnostic sect] and others are today, in the Islamic State, a people of war not enjoying a status of protection. . . . If they desire security and safety they must create a new pact with the Islamic State in accordance with the conditions of the Pact of Omar that they violated."

Contemporary jihadists take pains to conflate Christians with their Muslim political and religious enemies—Shiites in particular. In 2004, the late Musab al-Zarqawi, then-leader of the Islamic State of Iraq, directly linked Christians to the Shiite government in Baghdad. "If the Muslims defeat the Christians and polytheists, this causes distress among the Shiites. And if the polytheists and Christians beat the Muslims, this occasions a holiday and joy among the Shiites," he said.

"The Shiites are not Muslims," he went on. "They are a sect that follows the path of the Jews and Christians in lying and infidelity."

As the Arab Spring spread across North Africa and the Middle East in 2011, al-Qaeda theorist Mustafa Abdul Qadir Set-Mariam—known as Abu Musab al-Suri—declared jihad against the Assad government in Syria. He proclaimed an urgent need to stop "Jewish and Christian laws" from being imposed on Muslims in Greater Syria.

Assad is an Alawite, a sect that combines Shiism with other religious schools of thought. Suri argued that Alawites and Christians were in league to expunge "hatred for Jews and Christians . . . from Muslim hearts" and to make "all relations with them be perceived as normal relations." Alawite rule would also force Muslims to "wear the garb of Jews and Christians and emulate their fads, their hairdos, their gestures, their diet and drink and their way of life. It requires that Muslims transmute into Jews, Christians, apostates or aimless cattle."

In sum, the jihad cards have been stacked against Christians. They are allies of heretics and guilty of leading Muslims astray. They connive with evil rulers to keep true Muslims weak—a strange view of a community which by and large is politically powerless. It is not a great leap from these ideas, extreme versions of Islamic tradition, to the beheadings and expulsions that characterize today's Christian persecution.

Bold Islamic scholars, religious figures, and, if they can be found, credible politicians can counter the ideas of jihadist radicals. They should articulate their opposition not in platitudes, but in terms of those Islamic traditions that reject and militate against persecution. Those include prohibitions on attacking civilians, the indiscriminate use of weapons, and sectarian violence. Some of these limits were developed in times of stress and conflict that were no less alarming to Muslims than the present.

Abundant modern as well as ancient sources can be drawn upon. Jamaluddin al-Afghani, a nineteenth-century Shiite thinker, argued that Islam was not handcuffed by texts but instead is open to reason. In writings comparing Islam to Christianity, al-Afghani never used the word "infidel" or similar pejoratives. Along with a disciple, the Egyptian Sunni scholar Mohammed Abduh, he argued that jihad was meant solely for defensive purposes and rejected Salafi doctrines of jihad against infidels. Abduh promoted religious harmony. Both were modernizers writing during a colonial period that was no less traumatic for Muslims than the stagnation and crises of today.

In the twentieth century, a variety of Muslim thinkers argued for a moderate Islam. Syrian writer Muhammad Shahrur imagined an Islam based on reason and belittled those who relied solely on holy texts as a foundation for law. "Jurisprudence in the name of God," he wrote, "is a farce that benefits only those wanting to maintain political power."

Syrian-born Jawdat Said told Muslims and non-Muslims alike that "You cannot go on living on the basis of the law of the jungle." In arguing against violent jihad he wrote, "Those who use compulsion are virtually calling others to use compulsion." The Egyptian lawyer and Islamic scholar Khalil Abdul Karim attacked Salafism for its belief that the earliest history of Islam was perfect and that nothing since matters.

These voices are rarely heard or debated widely today. They don't project the fashionable certainty of Good vs. Evil that dominates all sides of the debate over Holy Land violence. Perhaps the most striking achievement of the radical jihadists is that their philosophy has become a prominent reference point of Islam among Muslims and non-Muslims alike. That benefits only warmongers, to the detriment of Christians and Muslims.

3/ IRAQ: THE LAST MASS

Thy shepherds slumber, O king of Assyria: thy nobles shall dwell in the dust: thy people is scattered upon the mountains, and no man gathereth them.

—Nahum 3:18

On July 17, 2003, a Christian man by the name of Husam George Tobeya was shot dead at a Baghdad gas station. It seemed at the time to be an isolated incident, one drop in a tsunami of violence that followed the overthrow of Saddam Hussein in April. Sunni Muslim guerrillas were already bedeviling American occupation forces with ambushes. Terrorist backers of Saddam were attacking Shiite Muslims, who rose to power in the new Iraq. Car bombs echoed through Baghdad and other cities.

Iraqi police, holed up in their district offices, feared going outside. Crime was rampant and kidnappings-for-ransom became commonplace; it was especially alarming that many victims were children. Against this backdrop, the death of a single Christian man seemed to have no special implication.

In fact, Tobeya's death signaled the beginning of a rolling and eventually systematic campaign to terrify Christians out of their homes, neighborhoods, and the country. Christian persecution was to become an insistent subtext of violence in post–Saddam Hussein Iraq. It was a gradual process, not a sudden big bang of death and expulsion.

The campaign escalated year by year and into 2014, when Islamic guerrillas and terrorists expelled the entire Christian community from Mosul, Iraq's second largest city, and then towns and villages in Nineveh Province, the land of ancient Assyria. Christians lost their homes, businesses, and lives at the hands of Islamic fanatics on a drive to cleanse Iraq of Christianity. Churches, shrines, and even monuments predating Christianity were unceremoniously bulldozed or blown up.

Christians, who along with Jews are designated protected "People of the Book" under Islam, became peculiarly exposed to violence.

A narrow and selective interpretation emerged that took Christian persecution to still greater levels of ferocity. It held that Christians have no place in Muslim society, period. This is the message of Salafism and Wahhabism. Osama bin Laden belonged to the latter branch. Each sect views Christians and Jews, as well as Shiites and members of other Muslim groups, as heretical. The existence of these faiths contaminates pure Islam. Bin Laden's ideology was adopted by Islamic opponents of the US occupation and the Shiite government in Baghdad as well as by enemies of the Syrian government of Bashar al-Assad, an Alawite.

The US-led invasion of Iraq uncorked sectarian hostilities. The US and its allies failed to appreciate that Saddam Hussein's iron rule was not only a cause but a symptom of the country's historical sectarian rivalries. Iraq's Sunni Muslim minority had run the country for centuries and subjugated both the Shiite majority and Kurds. Saddam exacerbated tensions by favoring Sunnis over Shiites. When Saddam fell, both the US and the new Shiite establishment marginalized Sunnis, whether hardline followers of Saddam or bystanders. Instead of an integrated state, a Shiite-dominated, exclusionary government arose.

Christian persecution represented a cruel sideshow to the nasty Sunni–Shiite power struggle. From 2003 through 2014, Iraq's Christian population shrank from approximately 1.4 million to around 300,000. The exact number is hard to come by; Iraq's government does not consider the Christian exodus sufficiently important to monitor it with any precision. Christians have fled to Kurdistan (Iraq's autonomous and self-defended region in the far north), Syria, and Jordan, and as far afield as Europe, Australia, and the United States. Thousands have been driven from their homes possessing only the clothes on their back.

They will not return. Having been terrorized by insurgents and alienated from many of their Muslim neighbors, they see no future in Iraq. The 2014 mass expulsion from Mosul climaxed more than a decade of oppression, violence, and insecurity.

Clerics who experienced a decade of misery alongside their flocks have begun to argue against the pressure on Christians to remain in Iraq and keep faith with two thousand years of history. It is intolerable, they argue, to ask Christians to live in constant, existential and, so far as can be foreseen, permanent insecurity.

Mosul sits on a bluff above the winding Tigris River in northwest Iraq. Residents refer to the river's west bank as the "right side" of the city, and the east bank, the "left." On the left side stood Nineveh, a ruined city of Biblical antiquity.

Mosul once thrived as a commercial crossroads between the Persian Gulf and the Mediterranean Sea, but when the Suez Canal opened in the mid–nineteenth century, its mercantile importance declined. With the discovery of oil at the beginning of the twentieth century, the city again flourished. Mosul also lay at the intersection of regional groups competing for dominance: Arabs, Kurds, Assyrians, and Turcoman. Sectarian conflict was chronic.

Mosul was the Arab nationalist city par excellence. Townspeople identified with the Arab world to the west rather than the imperial Ottoman Turkish land to the north. Saddam Hussein, whose official Baathist ideology promoted pan-Arab unity, recruited many of his military officers from Mosul. His Fifth Army was based there. When the city fell into American hands and the Fifth Army fled, Baathist functionaries quickly organized to defend their neighborhoods against Kurdish looters.

For a while, US forces under General David Petraeus pacified the city with handouts of money, financed with loot from Saddam's central bank. But an undercurrent of resistance endured. Saddam's sons, Uday and Qusay, hid in Mosul until they died in a shootout with American forces in July 2003. In 2004, Mosul rose against the occupation, and unrest has persisted intermittently ever since.

Islamist groups played a key role in the resistance. Among them was Ansar al-Islam, a group that competed with Al-Qaeda in Iraq (AQI), which was an affiliate of Osama bin Laden's global group. AQI later transformed itself into the Islamic State in Iraq and then the Islamic State in Iraq and Sham (ISIS), which split from al-Qaeda.

In addition, former Saddam-era soldiers and officers created an Islamic-oriented fighting force, the "Army Men of Naqshbandi," transforming secular Baathists into Islamic fighters. Naqshbandi is a spiritual order of the Sufi branch of Islam that is reviled by Salafis and Wahhabis. Nonetheless, the Islamic State-Baathist alliance of convenience would spell the end of Christian life in Mosul.

In 2014, Islamic State and allied forces launched an offensive in the west central Sunni cities of Fallujah and Ramadi, which then spread north along Highway 1 to Mosul and the Nineveh Plains.

Mosul sits on the route from the Syrian border into Iraq. It is a bigger prize than the other Sunni cities conquered by the Islamic State. Fallujah, for instance, had a pre-war population of 320,000. Mosul's was two million. Nineveh Province also offered other valuable prizes for the rebels: oil and a dam supplying electricity.

The Islamic State was crucially involved in Mosul's conquest. Christians all reported seeing Islamic State guerrillas, including foreigners, acting in concert with veterans of Saddam Hussein's army. Witnesses told me that as far as the abusive treatment of Christians was concerned, it was clear that the Islamic State was in charge.

Boutros Moushi, a Mosul merchant, remembered hearing gunfire on the edge of Mosul as early as July 6. He didn't think much of it—bombs and shooting having become, by this point, unremarkable noise in the urban soundscape. "The wealthy had left Mosul early, back when they started killing Christians for working with the Americans. We had already had lots of problems in Mosul, so chaos was nothing new."

On July 9, Moushi saw that the Islamic State gunmen entered Mosul from the "right" of the Tigris River. "The city was paralyzed.

No one was on the roads. The left side was still safe," he said. On June 10, the Islamic State advanced to the left bank. "They set police offices and police cars on fire. We fled. Muslims, too."

In the pre-dawn darkness of July 10, Haifa Hazan, a forty-nine-year-old homemaker, woke up to a new city. Instead of the usual sullen, ragtag government soldiers in olive green patrolling Mosul, rebel militias sporting black uniforms and beards motored around in pick-up trucks mounted with machine guns. Men in Saddam Hussein–era uniforms took over government buildings and the airport.

"I don't know how they arrived, they just appeared suddenly," Hazan recalled.

Dawn clarified everything. The Iraqi army had fled. The Islamic State proclaimed the establishment of a pan-Muslim empire—a new caliphate. This alarmed Hazan. "I thought, 'This is going to be like Syria,'" she recalled. She had heard how Islamic rebels fighting against the Syrian dictatorship rampaged through Christian villages, beheaded accused enemies, crucified others, looted churches, razed houses, and forced Christians to convert to Islam or face death.

So Hazan, her husband, Said Nahum, and son Raed loaded their car with clothes and pans, and left. The exodus from Mosul included Muslims who worried that the new order would mean repression or, in the case of a counter-attack, Shiite retaliation.

The Hazans traveled to Bashiqa, a small village of Muslims, Yazidis, Christians, and Shabak, another minority. For a while the fear seemed exaggerated. The Islamic State and their Baathist allies pledged that Mosul would function as before. Some Christians thought this meant that things wouldn't be worse than they had been during a past decade of sectarian killings, kidnappings, and extortion. Hazan and family returned home on July 12.

For a few days, life returned to normal, albeit under the unsettling watch of bearded foreigners. Banners declared the creation of the Islamic caliphate. Women of all faiths were forced to wear a hijab, the headscarf used by Muslim women to signify modesty.

Then on July 18, the roof caved in on two thousand years of Christian life. Preachers in mosques set out three choices for the city's Christians: convert to Islam, pay a special tax, or leave. The entire population of about 30,000 Christians fled to nearby towns and to Kurdistan. "In the mosque, they said all the bishops had to go to a certain checkpoint, where there was a headquarters. They wanted to set conditions on us. The bishops refused to go," Hazan said. "Then they said it was permissible to kill Christians if they didn't leave."

Hazan and her family again packed their bags and drove to Qaraqosh, a Christian town in the Nineveh plains. It had already hosted thousands of Mosul refugees from the decade past.

Moushi also fled to Qaraqosh, but returned to Mosul two days later to be with his sister, who was tending to their ninety-year-old father. "On the corner near my house, there was a banner reading, 'Welcome to the Islamic State.' There were fighters from Spain, from Asia, from Britain, but mostly they were from Saudi Arabia. Baathists were with them, too. Many normal people had sided with Daesh," Moushi said, using the common Arabic acronym for the Islamic State.

On July 18, Moushi read a message on the Internet that said Christians must convert, pay tax, or leave. He, his sister, and his father left for Bashiqa on June 20.

In Erbil, I spoke with a furniture store owner from Mosul who declined to give his name, but who provided a similar account. "A Muslim friend called and said they are telling everyone at the mosque that Christians will leave and lose everything."

On Friday, July 18, at 10 a.m., he left, carrying with him only documents, gold jewelry, and money. Gunmen stopped them at a checkpoint near the village of Shalalat, near a waterfall. "Men dressed like Afghanis demanded everything we had. We gave money, but they insisted we had gold. Our women screamed so they let us go. The gold was on the women and they let us go." They went on to Qaraqosh.

Refuge would not last long in towns on the Nineveh plains, home to Christian, Yazidi, and Shabak peoples along with

Arab Muslims. Much of the area had been under the control of Kurdish "peshmerga" forces, the militia of the autonomous region of far northern Iraq. Peshmerga means "those who face death." The Kurdish forces evaporated as the Islamic State advanced.

Thabet Habib Youssef, a Chaldean Catholic church deacon from Karamles, remembered the Islamic State attacking his town on August 6—the Feast of the Transfiguration. "We could hear shooting. Seemed like nothing too serious. People asked me, as the head deacon, what to do. I said, 'Do as you think best.' I couldn't really tell them to stay. It was a hard decision. Within two hours, people started to flee."

Nineveh towns had set up civil defense forces to work alongside the peshmerga, but when the Kurds withdrew, the Christian militia also fled. "Everyone left, except me, about a dozen old people or disabled people and two widows," Habib Youssef said. "We stayed for ten days. Daesh people with rifles told us to convert. We refused." Such refusals became a valiant and poignant feature of the Islamic State takeover.

On August 16, the rebels gathered remnants of the Karamles residents in St. Barbara's Church, stuffed them into a couple of old vehicles and then drove them to a nearby Arab village. "We walked down the road until we reached an Islamic State checkpoint. Local Arabs were helping Daesh. People from the next village pointed out which Christians had money and who didn't," Habib Youssef said. "Daesh stole $800 from us."

Events in Qaraqosh, a larger Christian enclave, followed the same pattern. On August 7, the Islamic State entered and the peshmerga faded away. The next day at 2 p.m., the Islamic State fighters announced by loudspeaker that Christians had to leave. "We fled on foot. We walked seven hours until we got to a peshmerga checkpoint," said a woman who had first escaped from Mosul. "They took everything from us. I have no passport. I want to emigrate. We have survived for years, but I can't bear it anymore."

The outside world reacted with indifference. No one suggested military action to turn back the Islamic State. Kurdistan, the autonomous region in far north Iraq, opened its borders to the refugees but mostly left their care in the hands of churches and the United Nations. Few countries offered haven to the new exiles.

The international response changed when the Islamic State began to march on Kurdistan itself. The rebels had surrounded Yazidis, another minority, in the town of Sinjar, driving thousands to the barren hills. Only on August 7, the day Qaraqosh fell, did President Obama announce he would bomb the advancing Islamic State militias. He made no mention of the Christians.

In Qaraqosh, the old, the weak, and the sick were stranded. Aida Hanna Nour, forty-three, a mother of four, stayed behind to take care of her blind husband. "We were ten days in Qaraqosh.

We stayed because we thought Daesh would leave. There was no electricity and no water. We were afraid. We asked for water and sometimes they gave it, sometimes not.

"After a few days, they asked us to convert or leave. Then they ordered us out by a certain day. If we refused, they would kill us. We were helpless. But we did not want to convert.

"Some Daesh wore black cloaks. One was an imam from a nearby village. He pointed out who had money. On August 22, a mini-bus came. 'We will treat you well,' the people with rifles said. They were lying. They took everything, the gold, money, and documents, everything except the clothes we were wearing.

"Then a man in black grabbed her three-year-old daughter," Hanna Nour said, and burst out in tears. "He gave her to an imam, an old man with a long beard. The girl cried and cried. I said, 'Why do you take her?' He said, 'If you come a step closer, I will shoot you.' I went to the bus." One young man, who was twenty, and stayed to care for his parents, was also taken away.

"We were dropped at a checkpoint, then walked for seven hours. We crossed a river on foot and then the desert. I didn't care. I just wanted my daughter. When we got to the peshmerga, they gave us water. They then let us pass.

"I heard that my daughter is with an Arab. They want $20,000. My brother-in-law is in touch with them. We will give the money if we can get it."

Ghazala al-Najjar, eighty, was left alone with her sick and unmarried sister-in-law. "I've had five operations and my eyes are bad. We didn't have much contact with our neighbors and so I woke up one day and discovered everybody's gone. No one told us. The streets were empty. I went to the church, the door was locked. The shops were closed and I saw a Daesh man in black. I went back home. We stayed inside for four days. When our water ran out, we came outside," she said.

Al-Najjar saw three Islamic State men and one in a Saddam military uniform. "They asked me, 'What are you doing here? Why aren't you gone?' They gave us water. We didn't need food. The man in the uniform said we should go to the old people's home in Mosul. Don't be afraid.

"I said, if I am to die, I'd rather die here. Then three others from Daesh came. They were in Afghan uniform, but they were Arabs from Mosul. They had rifles and opened shops and stole everything. They filled cars with gas. For ten days, they pressured me to convert. I said, 'Dig a hole and bury me. I will never be a Muslim.'

"'You need to be Muslim to go to heaven.'

"'I don't want your heaven,' I answered.

"We prayed to Jesus and the men left. We found another stranded family. They had a disabled boy. They too were told to become Muslim. The mother of the boy told Daesh, if you bring your mothers here to be Christian, I will become Muslim.

"At 6:30, they took us to an Arab village. There, the Arabs treated us well and the village head asked a young man to take us to Kurdistan. We ran into a Daesh checkpoint. They asked our driver to bring all the gold from us."

An old couple, Delailah, seventy, and Najib Daniel, seventy-five, who said they had lived in Qaraqosh "forever," recounted a similar exit. "On August 20, they came to our house and told us to convert," Delailah said. "I answered, I don't change religions.'

"They put us, ninety-three people, on a bus. I don't know where they let us off, but then we had to walk for eleven hours. A boy carried me across a river. A woman couldn't go on. Another boy carried her on his back for three hours.

"My husband's feet began to bleed. Dogs came and bit at them. We walked and walked and got to a Daesh checkpoint."

At this point in her recollection, Delailah began to weep.

"They took the thing I treasured. My earrings. I had worn them since my wedding. Since then I had never taken them off. It was fifty years ago."

The 2014 expulsion of Christians from Mosul simply concluded a decade of persecution. The long process received little attention outside Iraq, but it was a constant feature of the insurgency.

Although supporters of Saddam Hussein spearheaded the anti-US and anti-Shiite uprising, their sectarian violence was for the most part opportunistic rather than principled. Baathist ideology equalized sects and ethnic groups under the overarching social category, "Arab." Members of all religious groups held positions in the bureaucracy; Saddam's foreign minister, Tarek Aziz, was a Christian. Persecuting Christians was not dogma.

The Baathist insurgency was driven in part by sudden marginalization. Youths whose families had been deprived of the privileges granted by membership in the Baath Party resented being excluded in the new Iraq. Jobs in the army and the police force, intelligence agencies and as teachers, truck drivers, and civil servants were lost as US occupation overseers indiscriminately purged Baathist party members from government work.

The United States occupation administration also countenanced a sectarian political system based on ethnic and religious groupings. In this system, Shiites would be dominant and Sunnis effectively marginalized.

As the insurgency developed, Christian persecution became a trademark of foreign fighters inspired by Osama bin Laden. A Jordanian named Abu Musab al-Zarqawi founded an insurgent group called Jama'at al-Tawhid w'al-Jihad (the Party of Monotheism and Jihad). Zarqawi was a Sunni Muslim, a veteran of the Afghan war against Soviet occupation and a disciple of bin Laden.

He had traversed Iraq, Iran, and Syria to establish fronts against the US. Besides the Americans, Zarqawi's other main targets were Shiites, whom he declared inauthentic Muslims who ought to be killed.

Zarqawi condemned Christians as Shiite allies. In 2004, he pledged allegiance to al-Qaeda and changed his group's name to Al-Qaeda in Iraq.

AQI was not the only anti-US Islamic group to target Christians. Another, Ansar al-Sunna, operated in central and northern Iraq and attacked both central government and Kurdish authorities, especially in and around the Mosul area. Ansar al-Sunna warned Christians to unconditionally abandon Iraq.

The US generally played down the early violence. Secretary of State Donald Rumsfeld dismissed the insurgents and their terrorist allies as "dead enders," the last gasps of a collapsed regime. Protection of minorities was never on the US agenda.

Even though Christians played virtually no part in Iraq's new political arrangements, they became a special target of Sunni rage as Islamists conflated Christians with the infidel invaders and with the Shiites.

This attitude was sadly ironic given the opposition of the Catholic Church and some in the Iraqi Christian diaspora to the invasion. In March, 2003, just weeks before the war, Pope John Paul II sent Cardinal Pio Laghi, a former nuncio, to Washington, to plead with George W. Bush not to invade. Cardinal Laghi warned that the invasion would open "further instability in the region and a new gulf between Islam and Christianity."

Exiled Christians sounded alarms. On the eve of the invasion, activist Glen Chancy wrote: "This may come as a shock to many Americans, whose image of Saddam has been framed by comparisons to Adolf Hitler, but the prevalent fear among Assyrians [Christians], both in Iraq and abroad, is that what comes next after an American invasion will be worse. Should the Assyrians be so concerned about being liberated by US military power? If history is our guide, they shouldn't be afraid. They should be terrified."

These fears acknowledged an enduring feature of Holy Land history. Since the time of the Crusades, Muslims have looked with suspicion on Christians when foreigners came calling with arms.

Zarqawi's butchery extended beyond Christians to Sunnis who opposed his cruel tactics. Even al-Qaeda criticized Zarqawi's violent campaigns against fellow Sunni Muslims because they eroded popular support for jihad. In 2006, Sunni tribes in Iraq organized in a movement called the Sunni Awakening and joined forces with US troops to oppose al-Qaeda. They helped pacify Sunni areas in central Iraq and freed American forces to concentrate on securing Baghdad. In June the same year, US jets dropped two five-hundred-pound bombs in a house near Baqubah in central Iraq where Zarqawi was staying. He died. Al-Qaeda in Iraq seemed, finally, to be in retreat.

But neither the Awakening nor Zarqawi's death ended Christian persecution. Al-Qaeda in Iraq went underground and survived. The organization grew in size, in large part due to the unwillingness of the Shiite-led government in Baghdad to reach out to Iraq's dispossessed Sunnis. The Awakening evaporated and the government refused to pay anti-Qaeda Sunni militias in Baghdad ("The Sons of Iraq"). The Shiite-dominated government of Prime Minister Nouri al-Maliki feared creation of Sunni militias. Many of the Sons of Iraq were former Baathists with military experience who, when the group disbanded, would join the Islamic State and provide it with combat training.

AQI gave way to the Islamic State of Iraq, which was led not by a foreigner but by an Iraqi, Abu Omar al-Baghdadi (though he may have been subordinate to an al-Qaeda member from Egypt named Abu Ayyub al-Masri). Both died in an American military raid in 2010. Abu Bakr al-Baghdadi, another Iraqi, took over the leadership.

The Islamic State joined the uprising in Syria and al-Baghdadi gave the group a new name, Islamic State of Iraq and Sham. After conquering Mosul in July 2014, he declared the birth of a caliphate designed to draw the allegiance of terror groups worldwide.

At least forty Christians a year were slain in Iraq between 2004 and 2014. From Mosul to Basra, they suffered shootings, bombings, and throat-slashings, according to a report compiled by the *Assyrian International News Agency* (AINA). Some Christians working for US forces, who valued them for their command of English, were ambushed and shot dead on their way home. Among them were four Mosul women who did laundry for American soldiers. Others were killed in liquor stores they owned. A Sunni gang in Kirkuk kidnapped Christian doctors to exchange for ransom.

On June 26, 2004, someone threw a bomb at the Holy Spirit Church in Mosul. If that anti-Christian message was missed, insurgents delivered a further notice on August 1, simultaneously detonating bombs at four churches in Baghdad and one in Mosul. The bombers were ecumenical in their selection. The first blast struck the Our Lady of the Flowers Armenian Catholic Church; the second hit the Our Lady of Salvation Assyrian Catholic church twenty minutes later. These were followed by the Saints Peter and Paul Chaldean Catholic seminary and the St. Elia Chaldean Catholic church in Baghdad, and, finally, St. Paul's

Chaldean church in Mosul. It all happened within a half hour; a dozen worshippers died.

Mowaffaq al-Rubaie, Iraq's national security chief, blamed the attacks on Zarqawi's group. "Zarqawi and his extremists are basically trying to drive a wedge between Muslims and Christians in Iraq. It's clear they want to drive Christians out of the country," he said. Between 2003 and 2014, at least a hundred churches were subject to car, suicide, and drive-by bombings, according to an exhaustive report by AINA. Al-Qaeda operatives warned Christian university students to stop attending classes in Mosul.

By 2007, entire Christian neighborhoods were under threat. Events in Dora, a mixed Muslim–Christian Baghdad suburb, foreshadowed future religious cleansing. On April 14, 2007, Al-Qaeda in Iraq took over a mosque in Dora and spread leaflets ordering Christians to convert to Islam, pay a poll tax to stay, or die.

AQI's entry into Dora coincided with the "surge" of US troops into Baghdad, during which four US brigades were dispatched to bring the capital under control. In September, General Petraeus reported that the goals of the surge were being met. The same month, however, an independent military commission headed by General James Jones attributed the decrease in violence in Baghdad to the Balkanization of the city, which had split into exclusive Shiite and Sunni enclaves defended by sectarian militias.

If the surge was working, someone forgot to tell Dora. The online *Baghdad Observer* reported that "elements of Al-Qaeda have moved into Dora from Anbar. No security forces are to be seen there, it seems to be abandoned by both Iraqi and [US] Coalition. In Hay al-Mechaneek people have been warned by these insurgents to uninstall the satellite dishes since this is 'Haram' [sinful] in Islam . . . . In Hay al-Mualimeen and Hay al-Athorieen . . . they are telling people to convert, leave, or pay jizya."

The *Los Angeles Times* provided this account of the attack on Dora:

"Gunmen began visiting people, making threats. UN refugee officials reported that militant groups also were demanding that Christian women marry members of their groups.

On Easter Sunday, the militants visited Abu Salam's neighbor. One of his neighbor's sons, in his early 20s, was sitting in his garden wearing shorts when gunmen seized him and took him away. A few hours later, they returned with the young man, wearing trousers, stole his brother's car, looted the house and tore up pictures of Jesus and Mary.

They left them penniless. A Muslim neighbor gave them some money, so they took a taxi and ran away, Abu Salam said.

The next raid came two days later, when a 60-year-old neighbor returning from a vacation drove up in his car. Gunmen pulled the man's daughter and wife out of the vehicle and then drove off in it. They held the man for almost two days and demanded a ransom. They cursed Jesus and Mary in phone calls to the man's wife.

After the man was released, the family fled, and the militants moved people into the house. To celebrate the evictions, the militants held a victory parade, driving their cars and waving guns.

'They thought no one could defeat them,' Abu Salam said. By the time the fighters visited Abu Salam on the first Friday in May, they already had been to the houses of his father-in-law and older brother. Abu Salam and his relatives were the last of 10 Christian families that had lived on their street.

Abu Salam left Dora within hours, but his father-in-law decided to stay and pay the protection money. That night, fighters visited the home. When his father-in-law opened the door, masked gunmen pushed him and demanded to know whether someone was hiding inside. They searched the house, looked for weapons and asked for his gold."

According to AINA, Hatem al-Razaq, an al-Qaeda imam, told Dora Christians either to pay him $190 or send one family member to the mosque to convert. Refusal meant expulsion from Dora and confiscation of property.

Fleeing families had to pay an exit tax of $200 per person and $400 per car to use roads leading out of Dora. Churches were abandoned; a Shiite militia battling al-Qaeda took over the Angel

Raphael Convent, which belonged to the Chaldean Catholic Sisters of the Sacred Heart. The Shiites turned it into their military headquarters.

A Dora resident sent an e-mail to AINA about efforts to get Americans to send troops: "We talked to many people within the American Embassy and Iraqi Government, but it seems nobody really cares, because they have done nothing . . . . Neither the Iraqi nor the US army has any activity there, and they have delivered Dora to insurgents."

Shlemon Warduni, auxiliary bishop of the Chaldean Catholic Patriarchate, complained, "They are talking about security plans and bringing peace, but nothing arrived in Dora. There are no rules, no government, and no government forces."

Mar Addai II, patriarch of the Ancient Church of the East, noted that, in Dora, "Only the families that agree to give a daughter or sister in marriage to a Muslim can remain, which means that the entire nuclear family will progressively become Muslim."

Dinkha IV, patriarch of the Assyrian Church of the East, which has its headquarters in Chicago, asked the Iraqi government to intervene and stop "Muslim parties and groups that are perpetrating violent acts against Christians."

Chaldean Catholic archbishop Emmanuel III Delly recounted that "Christians are killed, chased out of their homes before the very eyes of those who are supposed to be responsible for their safety." He criticized not only the perpetrators of attacks on Christians, but also the Americans, who "came to Iraq without our consent.

"God does not appreciate what you have done," he said.

The Shiite-dominated government did nothing. Prime Minister Nouri al-Maliki expressed verbal alarm, but centered his politics on Shiite supremacy.

In June 2007, Dora's St. Jacob's Church was attacked, two guards were killed and the building itself converted into a mosque. Dora's Christian population of about 10,000 was shrunk by half. By 2014, only 1,500 Christians remained.

Elsewhere, churches and Christian institutions remained targets. In 2008, AQI began to bomb churches on holidays. On January 6, 2008, Christmas Eve for the Eastern Church, four churches in Baghdad and a church, a kindergarten, and a convent in Mosul were wrecked.

The grisly war of attrition did not let up. On October 31, 2010, a group of gunmen from the Islamic State of Iraq parked a gray Dodge SUV near Our Lady of Salvation Syrian Catholic Church in the Baghdad district of Karrada. The men were armed with AK-47 rifles and bomb vests. At about 7 p.m., they vaulted the church walls. When security guards tried to stop them a gun fight broke out and two bombs detonated that demolished the rear door of the church grounds.

At least a half-dozen gunmen entered the church, shouting, "You are all infidels," and opened fire. The first target was a priest named Wassem Sabeeh, who was celebrating Mass. Bullets also struck and killed a second priest, Thaer Abdullah. One of the killers tossed a hand grenade into a room where about sixty worshippers huddled. Soon, a US helicopter hovered overhead and Iraqi Special Forces soldiers gathered outside.

At 9 p.m., Iraqi government troops stormed the church. The Muslim attackers blew themselves up, killing seven of the rescuers. Blood splattered the walls. Icons were shot up and tombstones in the cemetery outside damaged. In all, fifty-eight worshippers were killed.

The Islamic State in Iraq said it carried out the massacre in revenge for the rumored captivity of two Islamic converts in a Coptic church in Cairo. An Islamic State website announced: "Let these idolaters, and at their forefront the hallucinating tyrant of the Vatican, know that the killing sword will not be lifted from the necks of their followers until they declare their distance from what the dog of the Egyptian Church is doing." Survivors in the church said some of the killers spoke Arabic with foreign accents.

American forces would be gone by the end of 2011. The Maliki government made no effort to embrace the Sunni minority and end the civil war. No one paid much attention to the ongoing Christian tragedy.

In Christian tradition, priests are shepherds to the flock. This was especially true in the Christian Holy Land, where priests, bishops, and patriarchs not only ministered to spiritual needs but also served as ambassadors to Muslim rulers. Christian communities relied on the men in robes to present grievances to the authorities, negotiate taxes, and ease communal tensions. The clerics also relayed demands from the rulers to the believers.

Radical jihadists understood that if you eliminate the shepherd, the flock would scatter. So it came as no surprise that church leaders would be conspicuous victims of violence. To mistreat or kill a priest with impunity meant you could harm anyone.

The first target was Syrian Catholic bishop Basil George Casmoussa on January 17, 2005. He had been on a visit to a family in Mosul when a car full of gunmen, some masked and some not, blocked the road. Men seized him and stuffed him into the trunk of their vehicle.

Casmoussa told reporters he was treated well, and implied the whole thing was a mistake. "When they realized who I was, things changed and they freed me at about 12:30 p.m.," he said. "In such a situation, you expect the worst."

Like many church officials at the time, Casmoussa attributed the act as a symptom of anti-American fervor. "I don't think it was something anti-Christian. It was something done to get the Americans out of the country. There is no common ground between Iraqi Christians and the occupiers . . . . They accused me of being a collaborator with the Americans, but as we talked, they realized that I work instead for unity and sovereignty of our country."

Iraqis in general assumed that Christians were well-off and that they would pay ransom for their clerics. As a result, abductions-for-money grew apace. In July 2006, Fr. Raad Washan Sawa was kidnapped and released after a day. In August, Fr. Saad Sirop Hanna, a priest in Dora, was abducted and held for four weeks. The next month, gunmen captured Chaldean Catholic priest Basel Salem Yaldo and detained him for two days. In all cases, though payment was demanded, they were freed without paying, the churches announced.

In September 2006, an event took place in Europe which cemented a religious impulse for the attacks. Pope Benedict XVI had traveled to Germany to speak at Regensburg University. The topic was Faith and Reason. In the middle of his lecture, Benedict discussed a conversation between a fourteenth-century Byzantine emperor and an "educated Persian," during which the emperor said, "Show me just what Mohammed brought that was new, and there you will find things only evil and inhuman, such as his command to spread by the sword the faith he preached."

Though the pope noted that the emperor had spoken with an unseemly "brusqueness," offense was taken. Muslim preachers throughout the Islamic world expressed outrage. Christians in Iraq would pay a price, just as they would later in the 2010 cases of the Danish cartoons of Mohammed and the burning of a Koran by a wacky American preacher.

That's not to suggest that if the pope had said nothing, all would have been fine in Iraq. Al-Qaeda in Iraq was already busy vandalizing churches, shaking down Christians for money, and killing them. The pope's words were merely a pretext for escalation, albeit an emotive one.

On September 24, 2006, a horde of gunmen shot up the Chaldean Catholic Church of the Holy Spirit in Mosul. The church was empty and no one was killed. Someone plastered leaflets on walls throughout Mosul demanding that Christians repudiate Benedict's words. The leaflets read, "Christians will be killed and churches burned down." A bomb placed under Syrian Orthodox priest Ezaria Warda's car at Baghdad's Church of the Virgin Mary killed four bystanders, including a security guard.

In October, kidnappers snatched Boulos Iskander, a Syrian Orthodox priest, off a Mosul street while he was shopping for auto parts. The abductors first demanded $350,000 in ransom, which was later reduced to $40,000. They demanded that church officials renounce Benedict XVI's Regensburg comments. St. Ephrem parish in Mosul raised the money and parishioners put up billboards critical of the pope. The kidnappers killed Fr. Boulos anyway. They dumped his dismembered body in an outlying neighborhood, with his head resting on the torso and his limbs arrayed around it.

On November 1, someone planted a bomb that blew in the doors of the Clock Roman Catholic Church in Mosul, notable for its 250-year old clock tower. The three priests of the parish fled to Kurdistan; before leaving, they told Catholic reporters they had stopped wearing cassocks for fear of kidnapping.

Detailed accounts of torture and survival are rare, but I was able to hear an account of a horrific tale of kidnapping during a visit to Kurdistan in September 2014. It was from Fr. Douglas Bazi, a Chaldean Catholic priest who was tending to refugees in Erbil. He does not now look like a man who was tormented for nine days, deprived of water for four of them, had his teeth knocked out, his nose broken in six places, and his back fractured with a hammer. Surgery has concealed the impact of torture upon his body.

During a conversation at St. Elias Church in Erbil, Bazi narrated his story reluctantly—he hadn't publicly provided details before—and requested that I ask no questions.

Bazi had first been attacked in Baghdad in April 2005, when a gunman shot him in the leg. Then someone detonated a bomb outside an internet café where he was printing church fliers. Another time, a Muslim came up and queried, "Remember Saturday? It's Sunday now. Why are you here?" Saturday, the Jewish prayer day, was a reference to the flight of Iraqi Jews from the 1920s onward; Sunday suggested that Christians were next to go.

So it was not astonishing when, on November 19, 2006, Bazi was kidnapped while driving from his church.

"They came to the car and put guns at the window," he said. "They put me in the back of the car and after twenty minutes said, 'We are going to give you a scarf. You should put it on your eyes. If you look, we are going to kill you.'

"They kneed me and I felt a lot of blood flow from my nose. They took my ID and said, 'You are a priest.'

"'Yes I am,' I answered.

"They said they were looking for someone else. But in fact, they talked only about me. They took me to a room in a small house. In the evening they turned on the Koran TV channel loud, to show the neighbors they are religious. They also said, 'When we beat you, the neighbors will not hear.'

"They said they would ask $1 million in ransom for me and I laughed. 'If you catch Allawi [a reference to an opposition politician] maybe you can get a million.' They beat me.

"I said, 'You say you are religious but you are just a stupid gang.'

"In two days, they phoned a priest to negotiate. Then they stopped giving me water. For four days! 'You want to have water?' they asked me over and over. Each time I answered, they beat me and used bad words.

"On the fifth day, they brought me water.

"One asked me, 'Who do you think we are?' I said I believe that if you had a chance, you might be a doctor, an engineer, but you are being used because you are poor.

"They were silent. Then minutes later, one sat on each side of me and began to tell me their problems. One said that Saddam took his house. By day, they asked me advice. By night, they beat me.

"They told me, 'It's nothing personal. We have a list of targets for money." They said, 'Look, we have walkie-talkies, police cars, ambulances, checkpoints. Now you understand who we are.'

"One wore perfume and a leather jacket. He knew police interrogation techniques." 'Just cooperate,' he advised me.

"They told me they were going to cut off my head and replace it with a dog's. I laughed, I don't know why.

"'We will slice your body parts and hit you with the pieces.'

"I said, 'I'd be dead so why bother? For us Christians, death is a beginning.' "If you kill me, you are not men. You won't kill me because you can't.'

"On November 6, they negotiated with a priest at my church. The priest said, 'We don't need him. He will be a martyr. Keep him.'

"So they took me and shouted, 'Bring a hammer.' I was soon all bloody. They broke my teeth.

"Your friends don't need you! they said.

"I'm happy, I answered

"'Why not beg for your life?' And they hit me with a hammer on the left front shoulder.

"I said, 'Make it fast.' And they said, 'We have all night.'

"They used pliers. And a cigar. And insulted my family. I didn't look to survive. To die would be a miracle.

"I lost my nose, then teeth. I was hit with a hammer on the lower back. They brought me tea. By then, I couldn't drink tea, but according to Muslim tradition, they have to take care of you. Be hospitable."

"I said, 'I am not your enemy. Go and fight the US, not civilians.'"

"I was chained and I used the chain as a rosary and to count the days. I asked for books. 'Who told you we have books?' they wondered.

"They asked if I would take revenge." I said, 'I will remember but not avenge.'

"'You are stupid,' they said.'"

One day, the kidnappers put Bazi in in women's clothing and brought him shoes that were not his. They put him in a car. "I thought it was the end," Bazi recalled.

"Two voices I heard were not nice. Another was calm, next to me, and whispered, 'Don't say anything.'

"We stopped and they said jump out.

"I waited to hear the shot."

There was no shot.

The car left and Bazi wandered on a highway. He hailed a taxi to his old neighborhood. He found Fr. Jamil, a colleague.

"He had been told I'd be around. I cried.

"'Now you are in our hands,' Jamil said. "I told him I wanted to go to my church. It was 10 p.m."

The parish had paid the kidnappers $85,000 in ransom money.

Bazi stayed in Baghdad until Christmas to fix his nose. He joked with doctors that he wanted one like Nancy Agram, a sexy Lebanese singer who herself was a veteran of cosmetic surgery.

Surgeons in Italy repaired his teeth and, in Germany, his broken spine. The damaged back kept him in bed one year. He needed crutches to stand. Doctors eventually put screws and a plate in his back to fix it.

"While I was gone from Iraq, I felt guilty," he told me. "What of the people I left? It gave me a new view of life. I'm not a hero. I was just lucky."

Then he ended his tale: "I always keep a bottle of water at my bedside."

Other clerical victims would not survive. Three days after Bazi was kidnapped, Elder Munthir al-Saqa, a preacher from Mosul's Presbyterian Church, disappeared. Kidnappers wanted $1 million in ransom. The sum was unattainable. Six days later, Saqa's body was found in the street with a bullet through his head.

Around the same time, a Chaldean Catholic priest named Ragheed Aziz Ganni wrote an alarming note to a friend in Rome, where he had been a seminarian, to relate the downward spiral of Christian life in Mosul.

"The Pope's speech lit a fire in the city. A Syrian Orthodox priest was beheaded; my parish church was attacked five times. I was threatened even before that priest was kidnapped, but I was very careful about moving around. I postponed my vacation twice because I couldn't leave the city under such conditions. I was planning to travel to Europe on September 18, but I moved it to October 4. Then I had to change the date to November 1. "Ramadan was a disaster for us in Mosul," Ganni went on. "Hundreds of Christian families fled outside the city including my family and uncles. About 30 people left all their properties and fled, having been threatened."

Speaking to AsiaNews, a Catholic news service, he described the danger to Christian worship in Mosul: "The young people organized surveillance after the recent attacks against the parish, the kidnappings, the threats . . . . Priests celebrate Mass amidst the bombed-out ruins; mothers worry as they see their children challenge danger to attend catechism with enthusiasm; the elderly come to entrust their fleeing families to God's protection; they alone remain in their country where they have their roots and built their homes, refusing to flee. Exile for them is unimaginable."

On May 28, 2007, he e-mailed a friend: "We are on the verge of collapse."

Five days later, Ganni left the Holy Spirit Church for home in a car with one of his sub deacons, Basman Yusef Daoud, after celebrating Mass. Sub deacons are ordained positions below deacons in the Chaldean church. Ganni was followed in another vehicle by two other sub deacons, Gassan Issam Bidaed and Wahid Hanna Isho, along with Isho's wife, Bayan Adam Bella. Only Bella survived the trip. She described the horror to AsiaNews, a Catholic agency:

"At a certain point, the car was stopped by armed men. Father Ragheed could have fled, but he did not want to because he knew they were looking for him," she said, meaning that Ganni thought he was the target of the kidnappers.

"They forced us to get out of the car and led me away. Then one of the killers screamed at Father Ragheed, 'I told you to close the church. Why didn't you do it? Why are you still here?'

"And he simply responded, 'How can I close the house of God?'"

"They immediately pushed him to the ground, and Father Ragheed had only enough time to gesture to me with his head that I should run away. Then they opened fire and killed all four of them.

"Why did they make me a widow? Why did they tear the word 'papa' from the mouths of my children? What did we do wrong? What did my husband do?"

After the shooting, the killers placed explosives in Ganni's car to deter anyone from approaching. The corpses were recovered late that night after a bomb squad arrived.

Ragheed was buried in his hometown of Karamles near Mosul. Paulos Faraj Rahho, the Chaldean Catholic archbishop of Mosul, presided and read a message from Pope Benedict, who appealed for all "to reject the ways of hatred and violence, to conquer evil with good and to cooperate in hastening the dawn of reconciliation, justice, and peace in Iraq."

During the 2007 US "surge," Rahho noted that Mosul had become more dangerous as American troops moved south to Baghdad. He told AsiaNews: "Of course, everyone is suffering from this war, irrespective of religious affiliation, but in Mosul, Christians face starker choices. Short of fleeing, they can choose between converting to Islam, paying the jizya, or death. Terrorists are behind intimidations and actions . . . but so are common criminals who use Islam to get rich. In the meantime, only one Christian in three is left in the city."

Bishop Rahho would soon be dead.

Gunmen captured him as he left the Holy Spirit Church after Mass on February 29, 2008. He was traveling in a car with a pair of bodyguards and his driver. The gunmen drenched the car in bullets. Only Rahho survived the fusillade. The kidnappers stuffed him into the trunk of their car and sped away.

While in the trunk, Rahho used his cell phone to call his church and request that no one pay ransom, as it would be used to fund more atrocities. A few days later, the kidnappers called to demand $2.5 million and for Christians to form a militia to fight the Americans.

On March 13, residents of an outlying Mosul neighborhood found Rahho's body, dumped by kidnappers in a shallow grave near Mosul. They recognized his decomposing cadaver by his beard. The body bore no signs of violence; he may have died of a heart attack.

A month later in Baghdad, gunmen using silencers shot down Youssef Adel, a Syriac Orthodox priest, in front of his home in Baghdad.

US officials and the Iraqi government uttered the usual assurances. The Bush Administration said that it would work to protect all Iraqis. President Maliki promised the kidnappers and killers would not escape justice. Of course, they did.

Through all this mayhem, it became ever more clear that a systematic campaign was underway. Christians and other observers, some of whom at first opposed the US invasion, now wondered how a US pullout would affect a fractured Iraq and its Christians.

After Ganni's murder, George Weigel, a veteran Vatican observer, wrote from Washington: "The Holy See's opposition to the use of force in Iraq in March 2003 is well known. Perhaps less well known is the widespread conviction in the Vatican today that a precipitous American withdrawal from Iraq would be the worst possible option from every point of view, including that of morality.

"Senior officials of the Holy See with whom I discussed the issue in May share the view of American analysts who are convinced that a premature American disengagement from Iraq would lead to genocidal violence, Iraq's collapse into a failed state, chaos throughout the Middle East, and a new haven for international terrorists. That all of this would make life intolerable for Iraq's remaining Christians is pluperfectly obvious."

On September 10, 2014, during a speech heralding the bombing of the Islamic State in both Iraq and Syria, Obama finally mentioned the Christians and other banished minorities. "We cannot allow these communities to be driven from their ancient homelands," he said.

But they have been. I spoke with dozens of refugees who streamed into Kurdistan, as well as church leaders. All said that it was over for Christians in Iraq. For them, the expulsion was not the beginning of a terrible persecution but the finale.

A furniture store owner from Mosul put the matter succinctly. "Our bishops have been fooling us. They say that we must stay to save Christianity in Iraq. Forget about it. Christianity is dead in Iraq."

Douglas Bazi asked, "Stay to prove what? What is it to remain if you cannot worship, if you are forced to pay special taxes? If you can't live in dignity? Our bishops are fooling us and themselves by urging people to stay. If we live the same life in Mosul and around it as before, we will remain enslaved. Iraq is not for Christians anymore."

Mar Nicodemus Dawood Matti Sharaf, the Syriac Orthodox bishop of Mosul, Kirkuk, and Kurdistan, concurred. "There are no human rights for Eastern Christians. I have no faith in human rights work. The Islamists have taken our dignity, our history.

"We only think about a chance to leave. One year, maybe two maximum, there will be no Christians in Iraq."

For the first time since the thirteenth century, when Mongol invaders razed the city to quell an uprising, Mosul's Christian worship has fallen silent. The final Mass was performed in Mosul churches on July 9, 2014.

4/ SYRIA: APOCALYPSE NOW

God has guaranteed me Sham and its people.

—Quotation attributed to the Prophet Mohammed

The carnage in Syria cannot be classified simply as a war on Christianity. It is, rather, war of all against all.

Much of the country's majority Sunni Muslim population is in revolt against the government of Bashar al-Assad. On the other side stand Assad's supporters: the Alawite community, an offshoot of Shiite Islam to which Assad belongs; the Sunni middle class centered in Damascus, Aleppo, and major other cities; and Christians concentrated in Damascus, Aleppo, Homs, and smaller towns. A Kurdish population is also engaged, though largely because it harbors separatist aspirations in the far north.

The suffering has been immense, especially among the Sunni communities arrayed against the government. Though in recent months atrocities by the Islamic State have garnered much publicity, overall, Assad's forces have been responsible for the vast majority of civilian casualties.

As of 2015, at least 200,000 people have died in the war, according to the United Nations. At least 73,000 have been civilians have been killed. Of Syria's population of 22 million, 3 million have fled to neighboring countries and Europe while more than 6 million are displaced from their homes and living elsewhere inside Syria. The Assad regime's atrocities include indiscriminate bombing of civilian neighborhoods, deployment of chemical weapons, and sieges to induce hunger. Sunni rebel abuses are also rampant, and include mass killings, summary executions, stoning, crucifixions, beheadings, and the throwing of gay men off rooftops.

To say that Christians are not the only target of civil war violence does not mean that Christian communities are not in particular existential danger. Christians face a perilous future regardless of the civil war's outcome. If Assad loses, they will likely be persecuted by a vengeful insurgency as collaborators. If Assad forces prevail, their future will remain precarious in an embittered Sunni-majority country.

Syrian Christians numbered as many as 1.4 million before the civil war. The largest community was Greek Orthodox but the population included Greek Catholics, members of the Armenian Apostolic Church, the Syriac Orthodox Church, the Assyrian Church of the East and churches linked to Roman Catholicism—the Melkite Greek Catholic Church, the Syriac Maronite Church of Antioch, the

Armenian Catholic Church, the Syrian Catholic Church and the Chaldean Catholic Church. Under the Baathist governments, they possessed relative religious freedom. They could easily repair and build churches and hold public celebrations. Their state identity cards made no mention of their faith, although personal status laws, such as those concerning marriage, were left to individual religious communities. Christian holidays were official state days off.

Syrian Christians practiced the traditional pursuits of minority populations, engaging in commerce, craftsmanship, and skilled labor and professions. Many prospered. After the nationalization of businesses in the 1960s, middle-class Christians fled in large numbers. Education was an important value in the community and well-off Christians regarded the closure of Christian private schools in 1969 as a blow to their prospects in Syria. Assad shut down the schools because he considered their existence alien to officially non-sectarian Syria. Moreover, students were being taught English and French by foreign teachers who might also spread dangerous ideas of individual rights.

Christians shared with their Muslim co-nationalists the discomfort of living under Assad's police state. Clergy were expected to pledge loyalty to the regime and stay out of politics, and the intelligence services kept tabs on all without discrimination. In the civil war that has now engulfed their country, Syrian Christians and Muslims alike have been dragged in whether partisan or not.

In part, Christian fate now rests in the hands of radical jihadists, the most militant and militarily successful of rebel groups. These organizations have singled out Christians not only as supporters of the Assad regime, but as unfit to live in Syria under any circumstances short of total subservience.

Contemporary jihad aspires to create a pure Islam free of outside influence in order to assure Muslim ascendancy and Islam's eventual triumph worldwide. In particular, the Islamic State holds an apocalyptic view of the global stakes: as foreordained in the Koran, a climactic battle with infidel forces will usher in the End of Days. In the Islamic State's peculiar scenario, the Christian role is to be driven out in advance. It is this zealous concept that distinguishes current radical jihad from the framework of past holy wars.

For Christians in Syria, apocalypse is now.

In its early days, the anti-Assad uprising had little to do with radical jihad, much less the End of Days. It began with anti-government demonstrations that even Christians could—and did— join. In March 2011, anti-Assad protests were of a piece with Arab Spring pro-democracy movements sweeping the region. Protests in Tunisia and Egypt showed that dictatorships could be overthrown. In Syria, a concrete domestic crisis also motivated the demonstrators: a five-year drought had driven hundreds of thousands of impoverished rural Syrians to the cities.

The government, enamored of laissez faire capitalism and complacent among the new, trendy restaurants of Damascus, paid scant attention to the calamity. Two years into the drought—at its height!—Assad cut fuel and agricultural subsidies, making already difficult hardscrabble farming more expensive.

As displaced rural populations drifted into cities, the government responded by keeping images of destitute peasants out of newspapers and off television screens.

The first protests broke out in the southern town of Deraa, an agricultural market center hard hit by drought. At first, townsfolk demanded only the release of children who had been arrested after scrawling anti-government graffiti on walls.

The government reaction showed that Assad would tolerate no Syrian version of Arab Spring. Within a few days, soldiers had shot and killed fifteen protestors in Deraa. Demonstrations spread nationwide. Farouk as-Sharaa, the vice president, quickly labeled the unrest the work of al-Qaeda and of Afghanistan's Taliban. Both, he said, were in league with the United States—odd as that combination sounds.

Sectarian resentments emerged quickly. Deraa is a Sunni-majority city and some demonstrators chanted, "No Iran. No Hezbollah. We want a Muslim who fears God" —this latter phrase was used decades before by the Muslim Brotherhood to besmirch the Alawites, whom they consider false Muslims.

Sunnis had long harbored grievances over second-class status under the Assad dynasty and toward its Alawite backers. Though nominally at the head of a non-sectarian government, the Assads packed security services with Alawites and made them an object of hate beyond the issue of their religious orientation. The Assads inherited a tradition from French colonialists who, practicing a divide and rule policy, stocked the colonial army rank and file with Alawites. The French dispersed other ethnic and religious groupings in other government institutions.

For Christians, recent regional history suggested that sticking with the familiar was a safer bet than risking all on a precarious future. Iraq was the prime exhibit. Soon after the United States–led invasion of Iraq overthrew Saddam Hussein in 2003, violence directed against Christian communities became a subplot in the Sunni–Shiite power struggle.

Tens of thousands of Iraqi Christians, as well as Muslims, fled to Syria, and the Assad government hosted them. Many Christians saw this charitable act as proof that Assad's Syria was a political oasis that welcomed and protected all minorities. The conclusion was somewhat misguided; Assad had also permitted Iraqi insurgents to base themselves in Syria, from which they launched attacks inside Iraq—and tormented Iraqi Christians.

The Arab Spring, meanwhile, looked like anything but a godsend. In Egypt, the ouster of President Hosni Mubarak gave way to mob assaults led by Salafi preachers on Christian churches and communities. Egyptians then elected a president from the Muslim Brotherhood, Mohammed Morsi, who strengthened Islamic law as the basis of Egypt's legal system. Hundreds of thousands of Muslims and Christians alike protested Morsi's authoritarian outlook. In July 2013, the Egyptian army overthrew Morsi—but due to their participation in anti-Morsi protests, Christians got the blame. Although many more Muslims than Christians took part in efforts to unseat Morsi, the Brotherhood encouraged an unprecedented wave of attacks on Christians the length of Egypt.

Assad ruled Syria under the secular ideology Baathism, which sidelined Islam as the guiding principle of political life. In the early 1980s, the Muslim Brotherhood led a Sunni revolt. It was crushed by Hafez al-Assad, Bashar's father, who ruled Syria for thirty years until his death in 2000.

Christians were integrated into some parts of the bureaucracy, even in high office. Daoud Rajiha, the Syrian Defense Minister at the beginning of the 2011 uprising, was Christian. In 2012, assassins from the Free Syrian Army, a rebel group supported by the West, blew him up at National Security headquarters in downtown Damascus. A Sunni general replaced him.

The rebellion in Syria confirmed the worst of Christian nightmares. Christians were killed and expelled from towns and neighborhoods, churches were ransacked, and Islamic law imposed on areas under rebel control. Eventually, Christians became targets simply because they were Christians. Patrick Cockburn, the veteran correspondent, reported in October 2015 from Syria, that thousands of Christian refugees have decided they can never return to their homes; they want to emigrate.

Faced with a choice between a rebellion, whose most aggressive and successful factions vowed to subjugate Christians if not eliminate them entirely, and a dynastic tyrant who devastated the country, Christians by and large opted for the devil they knew. An unknown number of Christian men have joined militias in support of Assad, especially in the western part of the country. Given the increasingly sectarian character of the revolt, the choice of whether to back Assad, in fact, was no choice at all.

Unlike the insurgency in Iraq, the Syrian uprising quickly became a battle for territorial control. In Iraq, an early effort to grab an entire city from US occupation and government forces occurred in 2004, when al-Qaeda insurgents and their allies took over the city of Fallujah. US Marines eventually drove the rebels out. The Iraqi insurgents held no comparable territory until 2014, when it captured towns in west central Iraq as well as the city of Mosul and its environs.

In Syria, on the other hand, battles over territory began soon after at the insurgency's outbreak. When rebels capture territory, jihadists exact bloody punishment on Alawites, their most bitter enemy, and also Christians. If government forces returned, Sunnis face danger and often flee.

In January 2012, insurgents drove the Syrian army out of Qusayr, a town on the Lebanese border. Qusayr controls arms smuggling routes from Lebanon and the north–south highway from Damascus to the major town of Homs. It was a mainly Sunni town, with a population of 60,000 that included perhaps 10,000 Christians. Paul Wood of the BBC observed the creeping sectarian violence when rebels, led by the Nusra Front, an al-Qaeda franchise, seized the town. Militiamen began to kidnap Christians, accusing them of working for Assad's secret police. Christians retaliated by abducting Sunnis.

Blame for the back and forth violence was pinned on foreign jihadists. But Syrian Sunni forces were clearly as involved. When Assad forces mounted a counterattack, Syrian Sunnis went door-to-door to expel Christian residents and ripped images of Christ from church walls.

When, in May 2013, Assad's army and pro-government paramilitary groups finally retook Qusayr, the process was reversed. Sunnis left and Christians came back.

During the same period, fierce fighting centered on the central city of Homs. A three-year siege by Assad forces ended only in 2014. Government aircraft rained makeshift explosives known as barrel bombs on the city. Rebels detonated car bombs. The Nusra Front told Christians to leave. During the siege, Muslim and Christian residents alike fled, though pockets remained to endure the bombardments and street fighting.

Among those Christians who stayed was Frans van der Lugt, a Jesuit priest from Holland, who tried to work out a truce. No one knows who sat him down in a chair inside a Homs monastery and shot him in the head. Nusra Front controlled the neighborhood at the time.

Christian clerics bravely tried to keep serving their congregants. In doing so, they faced abductions and death. Priests were often kidnapped for ransom, on the belief that churches and the Christian community had the money to pay. As in Iraq, the ability to threaten clergy with impunity delivered a fearful message to all Christians.

The attacks on clergy began early. In October 2012, Syrian Orthodox priest Fadi Haddad left his St. Elijah Church in his hometown of Qatana, southeast of Damascus, to negotiate the release of an abducted parishioner. The captors took him captive, too, and demanded money. Negotiations broke down. A week later, his body was found near a road; his eyes were gouged out.

In February 2013, Armenian Catholic priest Michael Kayal and Greek Orthodox priest Maher Mahfouz were kidnapped from a bus in Aleppo at a rebel checkpoint. Each was wearing black clerical garb. In brief negotiations by telephone, the kidnappers said they wanted money. Fr. Kayal was permitted to speak briefly to his mother. He told her, "Mum, I'm okay, but pray for me," according to a report in the *Catholic Herald*. Within two weeks, talks broke off and nothing was heard again from the rebels or the hostages.

Gunmen in Aleppo abducted the Syriac Orthodox archbishop, Gregorios Yoahanna Ibrahim, and the Greek Orthodox archbishop, Boulos Yazigi, in April 2013. They were travelling on a mission to free some hostages. The fate of the prelates is unknown. Some accounts say they are alive and in the hands of the Nusra Front.

In June 2013, Jesuit Fr. Paolo dall'Oglio, an Italian citizen, was kidnapped in Raqqa. He promoted interreligious dialogue and initially had been a supporter of the uprising against Assad. The Islamic State considered him a spy. Various third-party talks were held to secure his release, but nothing came of them. As late as January 2015, reports indicated he was still alive and in the hands of the Islamic State.

Continuous assaults on priests became the order of the day. Fr. Francois Murad, a Franciscan priest, was shot by Nusra Front in the Christian town of Ghassaniyeh on June 23, 2013.

In October 2014, an Antiochian Orthodox priest, Hanna Moussa, was captured near the town of Jisr al-Shughour, near the northern city of Idlib. On July 12, 2015, Fr. Tony Boutros and his driver, a Muslim, were abducted near Idlib, a town which is under control of multiple jihadist militias. All the victims have disappeared.

In May, 2015, a pair of gunmen on a motorcycle raided the St. Julian monastery near Homs and abducted Syrian Catholic priest Jacques Mourad. Mourad had taken part in negotiations to spare his home village of Qaryatayn from Islamic State rebels.

According to Aleteia, a Christian website, Mourad emailed a friend shortly before his abduction: "The situation is getting very complex. Men of Daesh are getting closer and closer. We hear that they cut throats of people of the villages nearby. Today we are still alive, but tomorrow is uncertain. Please pray for us."

In October, 2015, he escaped from the Islamic State. He told an Italians television station that he was taken to the town of Palmyra and held with dozens of other Christian hostages. "Every day someone came to my prison and asked me 'what are you?' I would answer, a Nazarene, in other words a Christian. 'So you're an infidel,' they shouted. 'We will slit your throat.'

Christian captives are still held in Palmyra, he said. The Qaryatayn monastery was demolished by the Islamic State in August.

As the uprising against the Assad regime gained steam, attacks
on Christians reflected the insurgency's increasingly religious
and sectarian nature. The jihadists' targets often made sense
strategically, but the rebels also found time to persecute Christians and sack their property for no particular tactical reason—
other than to remind Christians that they had no future in an
Islamic Syria.

In September 2013, jihadists led by the Nusra Front attacked
the majority Christian town of Maaloula, thirty miles from
Damascus. Maaloula lies on a mountain route to the capital from
rebel hideaways. But the attackers didn't stop at obtaining a mere
strategic goal. After routing the Syrian army and overwhelming a
local self-defense militia, the insurgents burned a convent, van-
dalized icons, and trashed and torched churches. The government regained the town in April 2014.

After Maaloula, the Nusra Front advanced on the town of
Sadad. Like Maaloula, Sadad was considered a strategic stop on
the road to Damascus. The conquest included assaults on Christian homes and shrines, and the wanton killings of civilians.

The attack began on October 21, 2013. The Nusra Front, the Islamic State, and allied groups slipped in from the Qalamoun Mountains on the border with Lebanon. They refused to let residents leave the town and snipers shot anyone caught out of doors. Of forty-six fatalities, forty-one were civilians, including fourteen women and two children.

The rebels also executed three policemen and two soldiers held in custody, Human Rights Watch reported. A rebel video showing four of the bodies announced that the men were "dogs of Bashar." The bodies of six civilians, including the two children were thrown into a well; all had been blindfolded and shot in the head.

One Christian man was used as a human shield and forced to escort a couple of rebels down a street so that government forces wouldn't shoot. The insurgents threatened him with death, reminding him that "We kill Nazarenes"—the name used to designate Christians.

Rebels trashed three churches and stole chalices, candelabras, and ceremonial headgear. They also defaced walls and smashed windows and broke down doors. On October 28, government forces retook the town.

In 2013, Monsignor Giuseppe Nazzaro, the Vatican's representative in Aleppo, presciently described anti-Christian incidents as part of a broader "plan" targeting Christian communities. He told *Middle East Christian News* that Salafi extremists and Islamic Front jihadists prevented the village priest from ringing church bells, forced Christian women to cover their hair, and imposed Islamic law on all.

Both the Nusra Front and the Islamic State justify their attacks on Christians as part of a revolutionary holy war. They are out to transform Syria into a pure Sunni state. This makeover requires the elimination of Alawites and other "polytheists," and also harsh treatment of Nazarenes. Once the destruction of heretic communities is complete, they will turn their attention to the behavior of Sunni Muslims who fail to conform to the radicals' strict standards of Islam.

The Islamist conquest and occupation of the desert city of Raqqa demonstrated the revolt's transformation from an uprising against a dictatorial regime into a movement for remodeling society. Raqqa was a majority Sunni town with Christian and Alawite minorities. In March 2013, it became the first provincial capital to fall to a rebel coalition, led by the Nusra Front. Later, the Islamic State militia arrived and for a while, the two groups ran competing administrations. After a feud with Nusra, the Islamic State took full control of Raqqa.

Abu Bakr al-Baghdadi, self-styled caliph of the Islamic State, laid out new rules for continued Christian life in Raqqa. He combined traditional Islamic treatment of Christians—they were being offered protection at a price—with demands for total submission. His list of restrictions included:

- No building of church structures.
- No displaying of crosses or biblical phrases anywhere, or praying out loud.
- No bells or anything else Muslims might hear that suggests an act of worship.
- No collaboration with enemies of the Islamic State.
- No Christian worship of any sort outside of churches.
- No preventing of Christians from converting to Islam.
- Express only respect for Islam and no disparaging of the religion.
- Pay the Islamic poll tax—up to four dinars' worth of gold—twice a year.
- Christians cannot carry arms.
- Christians cannot sell pork or alcohol in markets or drink in public.
- Adhere to "modesty" of dress and other Islamic rules.

Breach of any or all terms would put Christians in the category of people at war, leaving them open to execution under Islamic law.

It took no time for this so-called governing pact to unleash lawlessness. Jihadists stole crops from a Christian farmer. The kidnapping and murder of a Christian youth soon followed. A former Christian mayor of the town who had surrendered the city to the Free Syrian Army was deliberately turned over to the Islamic State, which spared his life only after he converted to Islam.

Vandalism of churches and shrines came next. The Islamic State set fire to the Melkite Catholic Church of Our Lady of the Annunciation. They removed the cross from the roof of the Armenian Catholic Church of the Martyrs and dislodged a bell, which they threw to the ground. They replaced the cross with the emblematic black Islamic State flag, used the churches as their private office and burned the library. Islamic State leaders justified these acts of vandalism with their particular interpretation of Islam. The churches were built after the seventh-century Muslim conquest of Syria and so were fair game for destruction. According to one Islamic State preacher in the town, traditional rules for sparing churches did not apply because the rebels captured Raqqa by violence. Within a few months, the Christian population in Raqqa shrank from around 3,000 to a few dozen, as they fled for internal displacement or into foreign exile.

The suppression of Christianity in Raqqa ran in tandem to persecution of Alawites and Shiites, for whom there were no salvation pacts. Rebels publicly executed three unidentified Alawites by firing squad. A video of the event shows a master of ceremonies decrying the "crimes of Bashar" against Sunnis and offering the Alawites as sacrifice to Allah. Each victim was shot by a pistol to the back of the head. In 2014, Islamic State sappers blew up a pair of Shiite shrines in the city.

Finally began the maltreatment of mainstream Sunni Muslims. The Islamic State prohibited smoking or selling cigarettes and fined men for failing to grow beards, Salafi style. They required women to wear veils. Shops had to close for prayer time. The Islamic State razed at least one Sufi shrine in the Raqqa area.

General prohibitions on all Muslims included the selling of Nike footwear and revealing clothing. "Be informed that those who sell these clothing items have sinned, just like those who wear these items, and the sin will remain until the end of days," an Islamic State leaflet warned.

A similar sequence played out in Idlib, and the area around it in northern Syria. The town was taken in March 2015 by a cluster of jihad groups led by Nusra Front and operating under the name the Jaish al-Fateh, the "Army of Conquest." Persecution of Christians spiked. Ahrar al-Sham, the "Free Men of Greater Syria," executed Elias Naguib and his son Nael Elias, a pair of Christians who owned a liquor store. According to the Assyrian International News Agency, Fr. Ibrahim Farah, of the Greek Orthodox Church, was detained by the Nusra Front in March, along with a local pharmacist. They were released three weeks later and Ibrahim, along with about 150 or so Christian families, fled Idlib for Turkey.

Before the fall of Idlib city, minorities in outlying villages fell into line. In January, Druze, an Islamic sect reviled by Sunnis and a community generally supportive of Assad, announced they had "converted to Islam." According to news reports, the Islamic State ordered Druze in fourteen villages near Idlib to implement "God's law" by destroying their shrines, putting proper mosques in all the villages, teaching Sunni jurisprudence, obliging women to wear head coverings and segregating boys and girls in school. Anyone who objected would be punished under Islamic law.

Idlib and the entire surrounding province are now ruled by numerous jihadist groups. Nusra Front is chief among them and has put Islamic courts in charge of policing strict social rules. But for the moment, the various jihadist groups can't agree on which Islamic courts reign where. They have had difficulty even agreeing on mosque prayer times. Nonetheless, the goal is clear: to set up a mini-caliphate of the sort already established by the Islamic State in Raqqa, with harsh restrictions on Christians and other minorities.

It should surprise no one that the killing, expulsions, and destruction have all but precluded reconciliation among Syrians.

Comments I heard from refugees in Lebanon who had fled Syria's so-called Valley of the Christians, a strip of villages near

Homs, were typical. Displacement and cruelties they saw had taken a toll on belief in coexistence. "We know that Sunni families will want to come back," said a resident of Qalat Nimrah. "They will want revenge for having had to leave and for the dead. That's the way it works here. We will be the targets, even if we say we were not with the government."

"There might have been a time," added another, "when we could have worked together, the Muslims and us and others, for some sort of democracy. But now, with Daesh and with the killing, there is no chance of that."

I spoke with refugees from Maaloula, a town particularly treasured by Christians. It had briefly gained fame thanks to Mel Gibson's *The Passion of the Christ*, a graphic retelling of Jesus' crucifixion. The film's dialogue was in Aramaic, the lingua franca of the Holy Land two thousand years ago. Because Christians in Maaloula spoke a variation of the nearly-dead tongue, it became a favorite spot for reporters to visit.

The Maaloula refugees were embittered, and not just because Nusra Front had shot up the town and rampaged through churches, convents, houses, and businesses. Sunni Muslims who were considered neighbors had joined with the jihadists, they said. Even before the rebels arrived "we began to notice a change in our Muslim neighbors," recalled Rita Haddad, a Maaloula resident and housewife. Local Muslims claimed the right to collect jizya, the traditional tax placed on Christians under Islamic rule. New mosques were suddenly under construction. They shook down Christians for money in return for permission to let them work their fields. High walls went up around Muslim homes. A small riot broke out over a petty grievance. "Little by little, we were distanced from Muslims, who began to move only in groups and meet secretly," Haddad said. "They were flaunting their superiority."

"Muslims began to block our access to fields and keep us away from the mountains. Something was up," recalled Thomas Khalal, a twenty-two-year-old son of a Maaloula baker.

When the September 2013 attack on Maaloula began, rebels fired on the city from above. A suicide car bomber blew up a Syrian army checkpoint at the lower entrance to the town. The army retreated on September 5, leaving members of the town militia—armed with hunting rifles and shotguns—to fight off the insurgents. The deaths of three Christians who refused conversion stoked panic.

"The rebels were shouting 'God is great' and waving black flags. We had never seen these in Maaloula," said Thomas Khalal, who took up a hunting rifle to fight. "I saw people I knew. Neighbors, encouraging them and leading them around town and yelling 'God is great,' too. Who can forgive that?"

Even Christians who, for self-preservation or out of conviction, tried to ease the belligerent atmosphere found themselves suspect. Rita Haddad recalled the story of thirteen Greek Orthodox nuns from the Santa Thecla convent who were kidnapped and spent three months in the hands of the Nusra Front.

They were released in exchange for several female prisoners from Syrian jails, and according to some reports, $16 million from the government of Qatar. "The nuns said they were treated well and even cooked for the rebels. Why cook for them? Better to have died and been a martyr. The nuns should be ashamed," Haddad said.

Analyst Aymenn Jawad Al-Tamimi, writing on the informative Syria Comment blog, summarized Syrian minority sentiment, including that of Christians, as of July 2014: "It can be seen that the trends among Syria's main minorities on the ground have yet to show any meaningful shift to the armed opposition . . . . The future points to the continuation of this general situation.

"The most important reason is the rise of the Islamic State, which has most notably imposed the second-class dhimmi pact on Christians in its areas of control." Dhimmi is a status of non-Muslims living under Islamic rule and who usually have to pay a poll tax and abide by certain restrictions.

Al-Tamimi concluded, "None of these developments can be seen as encouraging by minorities, and sadly indicate the continuation and aggravation of ethno-sectarian division in Syria for the foreseeable future."

Christians willing to speak out on Assad's behalf have been an asset in presenting his case in the West. For public consumption at least, they testify that the Assad regime, for its many faults and brutality, deserves to be preserved.

None has been more prominent than Mother Agnes Mariam de la Croix, one of the best known public voices of Christian allegiance to Assad. Dressed in her brown habit and white toque headdress, she became a familiar figure on Christian speaking circuits in Europe and the United States.

Mother Agnes harbors no doubts. Christians must embrace Assad as he has embraced them.

"Under the Baath, we are not ruled by Islamic law. We don't have much alternative but to oppose the radicals," she told me when I sat down with her in May 2015, near Beirut.

Describing a venerable survival strategy employed by vulnerable minorities in the world over, she added: "In general, Christians accept the authority in power."

Mother Agnes burst into media consciousness in September 2013, when she challenged foreign and rebel accounts of the use of chemical weapons in the Damascus suburb of Ghouta. The attack, one of the most horrific of the war to date, took 281 lives. Videos of writhing, dying children provoked worldwide outrage.

An extensive investigation by Human Rights Watch used satellite imagery, inspections of shells, and chemical analysis to conclude that Assad's troops had fired rockets carrying poison gas, including deadly sarin, into the district.

Mother Agnes disputed this. She said she had inspected videos of the dead and dying and contended that they were carefully edited fakes. She asserted that decaying corpses were stacked next to fresh cadavers and alleged victims were filmed in different places to reinforce the anti-Assad narrative. She said no one has produced names of the dead and that traditional public funerals weren't held. She then embarked on a foreign tour to defend the regime.

Her opinion made an impact, at least as far as rescuing Assad from international military pressure: Russia's Foreign Minister Sergei Lavrov cited her as a witness to a fraud. Moscow supports Assad and opposed military intervention. US president Obama backed off his threat to bomb Syria. Instead, he settled for a pledge by Assad to surrender his chemical stockpiles.

Before the poison gas controversy, Mother Agnes traveled around Syria with a hidden camera to get a sense of the rebellion. She mediated between the government and rebels over evacuations of towns under siege. These activities were bitterly controversial. In one instance, she was accused of tricking insurgent families into leaving a town and letting the Syrian army seize and imprison hundreds of young men. Agnes' detractors contend that she worked for Assad's intelligence services.

When I met with Mother Agnes she stood firmly behind her arguments. Assad was far from perfect, she said, but was preferable to the terrorists on the other side. The anti-government demonstrations that, at first, seemed to seek reform soon became a terror threat. "I quickly became aware of reality. I said, right away, it was the beginning of the sectarian war," she recalled.

Her biography depicts in miniature the broader story of precarious Christian life in the Holy Land. Her father fled from Nazareth during the 1948 Arab–Israel war. He joined a Christian militia in Lebanon, where he met her mother, a Lebanese. As a teenager, Agnes did a stint as a hippie and traveled to Nepal where she experienced a spiritual awakening. But, she said, she "never abandoned Christ." Her father's membership of a Lebanese Christian militia introduced her to Christian insecurities and sectarian violence.

She worked in the St. John the Mutilated monastery, a fifth-century structure she and her co-workers renovated in Qara, a town in western Syria. After witnessing rivalries between Islamist political forces and the Baath party, she sided with the regime. "The Baathists were tough but they brought us stability," she told me, before quickly qualifying: "I am not pro-Assad, and I prefer Bashar to the father. What I want has nothing to do with politics. It is equality I am after."

Nonetheless, she criticized Bashar al-Assad for economic mismanagement which, she said, had opened Syria to foreign competition and mainly benefited a closed circle around the president. She felt uneasy about abuses by his secret police, his pre-war opening to Salafi Muslim preaching in the country and the permission granted Iraqi insurgents to use Syrian territory as a base.

"I'm accused of being pro-Assad, but it's only a pretext. The fact is, Christians are being killed not because they support Assad but because we are not Muslim. The chants are this: 'Christians to Beirut, Alawites to the coffin.'

"The region is full of aggressive armed gangs—that's all they can be called—who want to divide us, who kidnap and behead. This is what is at stake," she said.

In 2012, Mother Agnes fled Qara convent under threat of death, she said. Secular rebels smuggled her to Lebanon. Even with all the bloodshed, she thinks Syria can be made whole again. "There is a social tissue that wants to live together, even with all the errors and the terrible security service misbehavior. People want a unified Syria."

At this point, that is hard to imagine.

5/ CHRISTIAN POLITICS: ACTIVISTS, TERRORISTS, WARLORDS

From champions of independence to Foreign Ministers, army generals to ideologues and government advisors to leaders of radical leftist groups, examples abound of Christian involvement in all aspects of societal and political life in the region.

—Fiona McCallum,
"Christian Political Participation in the Arab World." 2012

Although presently, Christians are rightfully portrayed as helpless victims, they also have a long and vibrant history of engagement and influence in Holy Land societies and politics. But Christian activism failed to head off their current predicament and their influence is fading.

Take Michel Aflaq. His mausoleum stands under a blue dome in Baghdad's Green Zone, a complex of Saddam Hussein-era palaces and buildings that was once the control center for the American-led occupation of Iraq.

Syrian-born, Aflaq was one of the most influential twentieth-century Arab political ideologues. He forged Baathism, a political framework for the region based on a distinctive Arab culture that, combined with traditional values and recollection of a glorious past, could fend off Western colonial intrusions and inspire progress.

Aflaq was Greek Orthodox. He aspired to erase minority subjugation through an Arab culture and common ethnicity that could override religious, tribal, or ethnic identities.

Indignities visited on Aflaq's tomb sum up the sad fate of Baathism. When he died in 1989, his disciple, a Baathist-gone-rogue named Saddam Hussein, used the occasion of his funeral to not only bury Aflaq but also Aflaq's anti-sectarianism. He pronounced Aflaq a Sunni Muslim and gave him a new name: Ahmed Michel.

After the 2003 invasion, up until at least 2006, US troops used Aflaq's mausoleum as a recreation room where soldiers on break from the car-bombings and ambushes that bedeviled the occupation pumped iron and played table-top soccer. So much for Aflaq's anti-colonial dreams.

I last saw the sarcophagus in 2010. The place was serving as a shopping mall for functionaries of the Shiite Muslim–led government notorious for the divisive sectarian politics that Aflaq abhorred.

Aflaq was far from the only Arab-world Christian political activist of modern times. In the twentieth century, Christian thinkers played leading roles in nationalist and anti-colonialist movements in Syria and Iraq. Christians in Egypt have consistently struggled for a society based on equality and civil rights.

During the 2011 Arab Spring uprising, young Coptic Christians promoted democracy and equal citizenship as the antidote to authoritarian repression and extremist Islam alike.

Palestinian Christians shared a fundamental experience with their Muslim co-nationalists that heavily overshadowed all other issues: dispossession of home and country by the State of Israel. For them, communal differences were secondary considerations, if they registered at all.

Only in Lebanon, a state expressly created by France to preserve its Christian communities (and French influence), was integration expressly shunted aside. Lebanon developed an awkward system of power sharing defined by religious affiliation—and, originally, Christian dominance. It has survived at the cost of civil war, constant tension, and revision.

Many Christian thinkers and activists considered themselves an integral part of the political and social fabric of the Holy Land and most could broadly be labeled secularists, since they believed in religiously neutral government. Some weren't religious at all. They borrowed ideas from twentieth-century European political fashions: fascism, socialism, and on occasion, liberal democracy. The secularists failed, and the failure has been a disaster for Christian communities.

The discrediting of non-sectarian political formulas was the work of many hands. Nominally secular Arab leaders—the

Nassers, Saddams, Assads, and Mubaraks—paid lip service to equality of citizenship but never put it into practice. Western powers dropped their attachment to civil rights at the door of the "stability" supposedly provided by these dictatorial regimes. Reckless Western military interventions exposed the failure of secular political leadership to resist. Humiliating military defeats by Israel further highlighted their ineptitude. The West's adventures also upset the tenuous balance of coexistence within the Holy Land. Christians were tainted by association with the aggressive outsiders.

Secular thinking put Christian political thinkers at odds with Islamist theorists who promoted an entirely different prescription for Arab renewal: the harnessing of Islam as a dominant force. In the Islamist formula, Christians and other minorities would revert to their age-old status as subordinate clients under Islamic law.

Ultra-conservative ideologies now command center stage in Islamic political debate. Beset by jihadist violence, and dramatically weakened as a political force, Christians today confront unpleasant choices: cling to the fragile shelter afforded by decaying and discredited dictatorial regimes, endure subjugation (at best) under Islamic rule, or flee their homeland forever.

Coupled with shrinking demographics and the rising Islamist tide, it is unlikely that Christians in the Holy Land will ever again possess the political and philosophical influence they possessed in the twentieth century.

The young Aflaq studied at the Sorbonne in 1920s Paris, when both Marxism and Fascism stirred expectations of rebirth and modernization in many tumultuous lands, including in the Middle East.

Aflaq toyed with both ideologies. Though Marxist in orientation, he borrowed rhetoric from the racial lyrics of fascism. His notion of Arab ethnicity emerged more from a sense of shared culture, however, than from visions of a Master Race. After World War II, fascism fell out of favor, and Aflaq and his followers airbrushed away their fascist dalliance and committed to socialism.

In Damascus, Aflaq founded the Baath party, got thrown in jail several times, and, on other occasions, fled into exile. With independence from France in 1946, Aflaq focused less on the nitty-gritty of Syrian life than on his overarching goal—creation of an Arab political union from the Tigris and Euphrates rivers to the Atlantic Ocean.

In 1958, Syria and Egypt tried their hand at pan-Arab unity by joining in a single republic. The marriage quickly soured. Egypt's Gamal Abdul Nasser, the charismatic leader of the most populous Arab country, considered himself the dominant partner. Syrian Baathist officers chafed under his bullying. Divorce came in 1961.

In 1963, disputes between Syrian Nasserists and Baathists brought on a military coup. Aflaq backed the Baathist putsch—he had already given up on electoral democracy. From then on, Baathism would be associated with undemocratic rule.

In 1966, another putsch took place. Military officers attracted by the economic possibilities and liberation rhetoric of the Soviet Union abandoned the quixotic task of building a single Arab nation. Baathists were excluded from politics and the military. In reaction to the military takeover, Aflaq fled into exile, first to Lebanon, then to Brazil, and finally to Iraq.

Yet another coup, in 1970, nominally restored Baathism to power, although pan-sectarian ideals continued to erode. Defense Minister Hafez al-Assad, the coup leader, established a secular regime. But Assad was an Alawite, which the majority Sunni Muslims considered a heretical faith, worse even than Christianity. To overcome this bias, Assad, with encouragement from Iran, got top Sunni religious figures to declare him an authentic Muslim. He appointed Sunnis to high positions and created an authority to build mosques. Still, to guard his back against the resentful majority, he stocked the secret police and other security forces with loyal Alawites.

In Hafez al-Assad's national order, Christians were free to practice their religion and carry on trade and commerce where they could. There were Christian ministers and advisors. You could believe in anything, so long as you did not believe you could take power from al-Assad.

Aflaq had left open the door to a measure of religious pandering. He was unwilling to embrace a fully religiously neutral state, which he deemed unrealistic. Instead, he promoted Islam as a unifying principle of pan-Arabism. He called Islam "the central cultural denominator of the Arab." In his manifesto "To the Memory of the Prophet," he stated that "Islam is a national culture," which Christians "must assimilate until they understand and love it."

Somehow Aflaq thought that granting Muslim cultural supremacy would turn Islam away from politics. He was wrong. From 1976 to 1982, Syria's Sunni majority spearheaded a major rebellion against Hafez al-Assad. He crushed it with torture, mass arrests, and massacres of civilians. In 2011 another revolt broke out against his son, Bashar al-Assad, who has responded with more than equal ferocity.

During his exile in Iraq, Aflaq saw his non-sectarian politics fully distorted and abandoned. Saddam Hussein appointed him head of the Baath party but gave him no policy role. Reporters who asked to visit Aflaq were told he was too busy to see them.

Saddam's Baathism was a veneer to mask the sectarian and tribal nature of his regime. His inner circle was dominated by his clan from Tikrit in central Iraq. The Baath party became a vehicle of Sunni dominance over Iraq's majority Shiites and the Kurds, the other major minority. Christians were, by and large, political bystanders. They saw in Saddam a tenuous, but perhaps necessary, barricade against sectarian violence. Multiple layers of secret police kept everyone in order.

A series of wars buried Iraqi Baathism. Saddam's Iraq fought a vicious eight-year conflict with Iran in the 1980s. He invaded Kuwait in 1991, only to be expelled by US-led forces. The United States led yet another invasion of Iraq in 2003, under the false pretenses that Saddam harbored a nuclear weapons program and had connections with Osama bin Laden.

The 2003 intervention broke Saddam's army and police state and set the stage for sectarian chaos that has yet to subside. Among the many victims were Iraq's Christian communities. Islamist rebels tarred them with being both agents of the West and conspirators with the Shiites.

Neither the United States nor the Baghdad government took steps to defend them. Remnants of Saddam's nominally Baathist Army joined with jihadist rebels to fight the Shiite government. Michel Aflaq's vision was at most a distant memory.

Westerners often wonder aloud why Palestinian Christians don't abandon the Palestine national movement and join Israel in an anti-Islamist front. After all, in Western tradition, Christians and Jews share fundamental values, which are set in contrast to the cruelties of violent jihad, which have been practiced by certain Palestinian factions.

Overlooked is the detail that informs most Palestinian Christian political thinking. When Israel established its state in 1948, Judeo-Christian ethics saved neither Christians nor Muslims from the fate of deprivation and exile.

This displacement makes Palestinian nationalism, and the Christians' place in it, distinct from the other such movements in the Holy Land. Iraq, Syria, Egypt, Lebanon all gained independence. Not so Palestine. Palestinians weren't focused on trying to resolve internal problems. They were trying to get their homes back.

Some of the most militant of Palestinian leaders had Christian backgrounds. Among them was George Habash, founder of the Popular Front for the Liberation of Palestine, a leftist faction of the Palestine Liberation Organization. Habash's organization was a pioneer in international terrorism and especially airline hijacking.

Habash and other Palestinian activists of Christian descent did not act in the name of Christianity. Their organizations were not structured along sectarian or religious lines. They were nationalist activists who happened to be Christian. "When George Habash spoke, he was not speaking as a Christian and he was not addressed as a Christian," recalled Adnan Barham, a former follower of Habash who first met him in Cairo in 1963.

Habash and many others were attracted to Marxism for its anti-colonial orientation rather than as a solution to Christian minority status. Habash's terror tactics were political tactics, not products of a lapsed faith.

In 1970, when airline hijacking was a major feature of the Palestinian fight against Israel, Habash told *Der Spiegel* magazine: "When we hijack a plane it has more effect than if we kill a hundred Israelis in battle. For decades, world public opinion has been neither for nor against the Palestinians. It simply ignored us. At least the world is talking about us now."

Habash was not the only Palestinian Christian theoretician of terror. A colleague, Wadi Haddad, son of a Greek Orthodox grain merchant, established an "external operations" unit to carry out terror attacks abroad.

Haddad launched the first airline hijacking in July 1968, while Habash was locked in a Syrian jail. The PFLP was a chief rival to Fatah, the top PLO faction headed by Yasser Arafat. In 1968, when Fatah forces held off an Israeli military attack on its base in Karameh, Jordan, the PFLP felt it needed to keep up. Gunmen took over an El Al flight that departed from Rome and diverted it to Algeria. The passengers and the plane were eventually freed.

From then on, hijacking and attacks on airports became common events. From 1969 to 1978, the PFLP was involved in thirteen hijackings and airport assaults. Cities throughout Europe were affected: Rome, Paris, Istanbul, Vienna, and Athens. In 1970, television broadcast the spectacular blowing up of three hijacked planes, one at an airfield in Cairo, the other two at a military airbase in Jordan.

The detonation of the planes in Jordan set off a war between the forces of Jordanian ruler King Hussein and the PLO. The Jordanians drove out the PLO and the group rooted itself in Lebanon, where it participated in a long civil war that broke out in 1975.

In 1969, PFLP members under the leadership of Naif Hawatmeh, a Greek Catholic by religion, split off from the organization and formed the Democratic Front for the Liberation of Palestine. The DFLP was also dedicated to terror; its most notable attack occurred in 1974, when a pair of gunmen infiltrated Israel, took over a school that sheltered over one hundred students on a field trip and demanded the release of twenty-three Palestinian prisoners held by Israel.

Talks failed. When a commando unit of the Israeli army tried a rescue operation, the Palestinians killed twenty-two students before being gunned down.

In February 1970, a PFLP spin-off, the Popular Front for the Liberation of Palestine–General Command, blew up a Swiss Air flight in mid-air. This was a dangerous innovation. Not only did it end the era of merely taking hostages, it introduced the idea of detonating a bomb automatically. The explosive was mailed to Israel, placed aboard the plane, and set off by a device sensitive to changes in air pressure.

Terminals and airline offices were not off limits to terror, either. In 1972, operating with the Japanese Red Army, PFLP members killed twenty passengers at Israel's international airport. Four years later, Israel foiled a PFLP hijacking in Entebbe, Uganda. That was the beginning of the end of PFLP hijacking.

Haddad and Habash split in the 1970s, in part because Habash opposed the attacks on non-Israeli targets and partly because the Soviet Union, at the time engaged in détente with the West, opposed the strategy of terror operations in Europe.

Habash's strategies exercised a major influence on the future development of terrorism and especially on tactics employed by contemporary jihadists. First, he understood that spectacular terror attacks could have a huge impact on the media. The 1970 detonation of planes on the tarmac outside Amman was basically a televised publicity stunt and, in its impact, comparable to the current jihadist use of online video to broadcast their triumphs and grisly executions. The tactics of both Habash and contemporary jihadists attracted foreign volunteers.

Moreover, the PFLP pioneered the idea of striking not just the main enemy, Israel, but also its allies outside the region. At first, the hijackings focused on destroying planes belonging to El Al (Israel's national flag carrier) and on attacking El Al passengers. Later, PFLP hijackers targeted European and American airlines and shot up European airports. Similarly, under the radical jihad of al-Qaeda, hitting the United States, Islam's "far enemy," was as effective as aiming at the "near enemy," Arab regimes that are allied with the US.

Habash's belligerency was rooted in the trauma of his family's 1948 expulsion from his hometown of al-Lydd, now Lod, near Israel's international airport. Yitzhak Rabin, later prime minister of Israel and hero of peace advocates, signed the evacuation order drawn up by David Ben-Gurion. It read: "The residents of Lydda must be expelled quickly without attention to age."

The eviction was brutal. As described by Israeli historian Benny Morris: "All the Israelis who witnessed the events agreed that the exodus, under a hot July sun, was an extended episode of suffering for the refugees, especially from Lydda. Some were stripped by soldiers of their valuables as they left town or at checkpoints. One Israeli soldier recorded vivid impressions of the thirst and hunger of the refugees on the roads, and of how 'children got lost' and of how a child fell into a well and drowned, ignored, as his fellow refugees fought each other to draw water to relieve their excruciating thirst. Another soldier described the spoor left by the slow-shuffling columns, 'to begin with [jettisoning] utensils and furniture and in the end, bodies of men, women and children, scattered along the way!' The forced march continued until the refugees reached the borders of what had been the Palestinian Mandatory."

Habash once told a reporter, "I was all the time imagining myself as a good Christian, serving the poor. When my land was occupied, I had no time to think about religion."

He began his political career as a pan-Arabist. He studied medicine at the American University in Beirut and got involved in politics at a time when Egypt and its president Gamal Abdul Nasser were the top candidates for Arab world leadership.

In Jordan, Habash and Wadi Haddad founded the Arab Nationalist Movement, which was funded by Nasser. Both were physicians and treated Palestinian refugees at a clinic in Amman.

With the devastating defeat of Arab armies in the 1967 Middle East War, Nasser's mystique collapsed. Palestinians abandoned faith in rescue by the Arab world. Yasser Arafat, head of the main Fatah faction of the PLO, considered direct Palestinian armed struggle against Israel as the future. The PLO borrowed tactics from the 1950s Algerian struggle for independence from France: terrorism within historic Palestine and attacks on civilians abroad.

Habash, along with Islamist groups, opposed peace moves. As early as 1968, a peace proposal put forward by the United States brought a sharp rejoinder from Habash. "We don't want peace! Peace would be the end of our hopes. We will sabotage all peace negotiations in the future," he said.

In the 1990s, Habash rejected the Israeli–Palestinian Oslo peace agreement, which he believed would eliminate the "right of return" of Palestinians to their homes. Rather than a two-state solution, he proposed a single state of Arabs and Jews from the Jordan River to the Mediterranean Sea.

Multiple dead ends of negotiations and the persistent construction of Israeli settlements in the West Bank eroded support for the PLO's leadership. Hamas, an acronym for Ḣarakat al-Muqāwamah al-'Islāmiyyah, the Islamic Resistance Movement, won parliamentary elections in 2006 and then in 2007 expelled the PLO from Gaza in a power struggle. Fatah held on to the West Bank.

The PFLP had neither the ideological heft nor effective tactics to remain influential. Islamist groups launched suicide bombings inside Israel and Hamas fought periodic wars with Israel. When Habash resigned as head of the PFLP in 2000, his old group took up suicide bombings but never regained its fearful reputation of the 1970s.

The conflict became increasingly defined in sectarian religious terms: Jew versus Muslim rather than Israeli versus Palestinian. The PLO itself began to encourage an Islamic identity in the fight for statehood. In general, the Palestinian Christian public was uncomfortable with the suicide bomb campaign launched by Hamas and by the PLO's al-Aqsa Martyrs Brigade. Christians preferred civil disobedience, but that was no longer on the menu of the PLO, much less of Hamas.

In an interview with a reporter not long before his death in 2008, Habash said it was proper to give Hamas and other Islamist groups a shot. Secular armed struggle, in his case of the Marxist anti-colonial sort, had failed. He told an interviewer: "We have tried, so let them now try. It is their turn."

I first laid eyes on George Ishak in 2005 on a Cairo street as he was being manhandled by a gaggle of riot police. He was leading a clutch of protestors who belonged to Kifaya, which means "enough," and was an umbrella organization of Egyptians who wanted to oust then-president Hosni Mubarak. Kifaya encompassed an alphabet of factions: Egyptians for Change, Writers for

Change, Physicians for Change, Students for Change, and on and on. It also represented formal political opposition groups: leftists, liberals, and Islamists, including the Muslim Brotherhood.

That Kifaya should have been led by a Christian—Ishak is Coptic—was of little significance in his eyes. He was uninterested in leading a sectarian movement of Christians on behalf of Christians. It was all about being Egyptian citizens gaining equal rights. "I always tell people, I was Egyptian by birth and Coptic by chance," he said. "Citizenship is what counts."

Egyptians have an enduring belief in law and the constitution, although neither has provided democracy, much less civil liberties over the past several decades. It's also common to hear Egyptians proclaim that theirs is a pluralistic society.

Yet Kifaya could not paper over the sectarian tensions in the movement and in society. That should have been no surprise given the sectarian nature of the Muslim Brotherhood, the largest and best organized opposition group. "Islam is the solution" was its lead slogan. Though it nominally backed Kifaya's efforts, the Brotherhood never supported equal civil rights for all. The group declined to mobilize its million or so members to take part in Kifaya's small demonstrations. One Brotherhood leader told me, "We are not extras in somebody else's movie."

Like Aflaq and Habash, Ishak's activism began during a nationalist struggle, not as a fight for Christian equality. In 1956 at the age of fourteen, he was at his home in Port Said at the north end of the Suez Canal, when British, French, and Israeli forces invaded Egypt. It was a colonial-style attempt to wrest control of the canal from the Egyptians, who had nationalized it two years earlier. Israel joined the declining imperial powers in order to rout Palestinian fighters from its borders.

The invasion, known in the West as the Suez War and in Egypt as the Tripartite Aggression, sparked patriotic passion. Ishak's mother wanted to flee. Ishak said no. He desired to stay and fight.

She agreed to remain, so as not to leave her son alone, but reminded him that, "If we die, it will be your fault."

Ishak roamed Port Said distributing anti-invasion leaflets. When the invaders withdrew, Nasser became a national hero. Ishak remained loyal to the communists, who had encouraged and organized the Port Said resistance. Later, as a result of the debacle of the 1967 war and dissatisfaction with repression in Egypt, Ishak fell out with Nasser.

Under Mubarak, he focused on liberal democracy and equal citizenship. The Egyptian opposition was always careful not to equate democracy with Western models. Demonstrations against the invasion of Iraq and Israel's continued violent standoff with the Palestinians presented Kifaya a cover for its pro-democracy protests. Kifaya preached democracy as a vehicle to strengthen Egypt and transport it out of the American orbit.

In 2003, activists met in a high school hall to plot the ouster of Mubarak. They agreed to lay out a manifesto but it took seven months to compose because of conflicting visions among the participants. Ishak and others insisted that Kifaya express itself in human and civil rights terms and avoid religious rhetoric.

To most Kifaya members, it seemed nothing strange that a Christian was their leader. "Never brought it up," Ishak told me during a conversation in Cairo in the spring of 2015.

In fact, his position was not out of the ordinary. Egyptian Christians had taken part in politics since the ouster of the Mameluke dynasty in the nineteenth century. Mohammed Ali, the first of modern Egypt reformers, provided Christians with business and government opportunities. Christians held high positions in the Wafd, the nationalist party that tried to end British colonial dominance of the nineteenth and twentieth centuries. In 1919, Egyptians marched under a banner that displayed an intertwined cross and crescent, a sign of Muslim–Christian unity.

Kifaya's innovations were many. The group held marches in defiance of government prohibitions and used the Internet to spread its message. The movement also exposed the impotence of traditional opposition political parties, which had all been co-opted by the government.

Kifaya's weaknesses were also significant. It remained an elite group that failed to reach out to the slums. Its eclectic membership failed to agree on the outlines of a post-Mubarak Egypt state. It eventually disintegrated over sectarian disputes. In 2006, Ishak issued a statement in support of the right of Egypt's Culture Minister Farouk Hosni to declare that the wearing of an Islamic headscarf by women of was "backward." The Muslim Brotherhood withdrew from Kifaya.

In 2011, mass demonstrations in Tahrir Square brought down Mubarak. A Muslim Brotherhood candidate, Mohamed Morsi, won Egypt's first post-Mubarak presidential race. Islamists also dominated parliamentary elections.

Political Islam's victories disturbed Ishak. "Like every other Christian Egyptian, I have fears. What we truly fear is targeting of the citizen's personal freedom. Instead of addressing what people wear, eat, or drink, why not talk about educational reform, or how to improve the health sector?" he asked.

He joined protests against Morsi and warned against new constitutional articles that imposed Islamic law on the Egyptian legal system. Ishak supported the overthrow of Morsi and the rise of army general Abdel-Fattah al-Sisi to power. He was unhappy, however, that the Coptic Pope, Tawadros II, stood in public alongside Sisi when Morsi was deposed and arrested. "This identification was too close," Ishak said.

After the violence that followed Morsi's overthrow, political repression intensified under Sisi's declaration of a war on terror.

Ishak's type of activism seemed fully in retreat. Not only did Sisi jail Brotherhood members by the thousands, but he imprisoned secular democratic activists. Guerrillas identified with the Islamic State turned the Sinai Peninsula into a war zone while assassinations of police and prosecutors keep Cairo on edge. The press is harassed and plainclothes police once again roam city streets.

Ishak still speaks out. In a long interview in June 2015, published on the state-run *al-Ahram Online* website, he said that the overthrow of Morsi and the return of the military to power were not meant to reduce civil liberties. He called for the repeal of laws that ban public protests and for the release of prisoners associated with the fall of Mubarak. "People demonstrated against Muslim Brotherhood rule because they feared for their freedoms, and it's mad that these freedoms should be compromised to the extent that we now see, under any pretext. It's really very depressing," he said.

As for the status of Christians, Ishak remarked that although Sisi attended Christmas Eve Mass at the Coptic cathedral in Cairo, the deed was no substitute for equality. "This is a symbolic gesture, but the values and rights of citizenship are what counts," he said. "The rights of Christians are at stake, no matter how good the chemistry between the president and the patriarch."

When, in 1936, Michel Aflaq introduced his pan-Arab ideology of Baathism into Syria, a young Lebanese Maronite Christian named Pierre Gemayel was attending the Berlin Olympic Games. Gemayel was impressed by Nazi Germany's goose-stepping zeal. A sports enthusiast, he was also captivated by a Czechoslovak sports society that combined love of acrobatics with patriotism.

On his return to Lebanon, Gemayel founded a movement and militia called the Kataeb, or the Phalanx. Its Spanish version, the Falange, was the fascist party that supported Francisco Franco in the Spanish Civil War.

The Kataeb clothed itself in the garb of Nazism—strutting around in brown shirts—but was mainly concerned with putting Christians, and in particular the Maronite Catholic community, in control of Lebanon. Gemayel wanted out of an emerging pan-Arab world. Unlike Aflaq, who considered Islam a benign influence, Gemayel was terrified of it.

France had created the Lebanese mini-state state led by Christians during its post–World War I mandate in the Middle East. The Kataeb joined with Muslim political forces to forge a "National Pact," which divided authority in Lebanon among Christians, Sunnis, and Shiites, with Christians as the dominant political confession. Thus were born the outlines of the modern Lebanese state and the source of its chronic instability.

From 1943 on, the National Pact froze the separate religious communities into perpetual competition. It seemed to work for a while. Post–World War II Lebanon was a place of vibrant commerce and sunny pleasures. Pierre Gemayel's belief in arm's-length coexistence appeared to have resulted in a happy ending.

But intense sectarian rivalries, not to mention violence among clan-based warlords, including the Gemayels, shattered this rosy outcome. The Maronites strove for total dominance. The Kataeb took leading roles in two civil wars. Competing sides shopped for outside support, including and especially from Syria and Israel. Warlords held sway throughout Lebanon.

In 1980, in the middle of a civil war that stretched from 1975 to 1990, Gemayel's son Bashir famously overreached. After much internal Christian bloodletting, he combined Christian militias into an organization called the Lebanese Forces. He looked to Israel to end Syria's interference in Lebanese affairs, to trounce the Palestine Liberation Organization that had run rampant in the country and also to perpetuate the political dominance of the Christian community, although demographically, it had become a minority.

In league with the Lebanese Forces, the Israelis invaded in June 1982. But Israel had its own overarching agendas: not only to kick the PLO out of Lebanon but to get the Gemayel to sign a peace treaty with the Jewish State.

Israel swept through southern Lebanon, bombed Beirut, and eventually occupied the capital itself. Although Bashir was having second thoughts about a treaty with Israel, things seemed to be going swimmingly.

Then a hidden bomb got in the way.

Seventeen days after his election to the presidency by Lebanon's parliament, an explosion at a Kataeb office in the Ashrafieh district of eastern Beirut buried Bashir Gemayel beneath the rubble and killed him and two dozen supporters. That set the stage for a horrendous revenge massacre by the Lebanese Forces. While Israeli military overseers looked on, the militia killed hundreds of unarmed Palestinian civilians in the Sabra and Shatila refugee camps in Beirut. It was a purely random vengeance. The Palestinians had nothing to do with the assassination, which was likely Syrian-ordered.

Bashir's short, fatal presidency gave way to the reign of his brother Amine Gemayel. Where Bashir was headstrong and determined to make Christians into a no-compromise powerhouse, the urbane Amine was sensitive to the need for reconciliation with Muslims. Nonetheless, he tried to seal a peace treaty with Israel, though the effort fell apart under pressure from Lebanese Muslims and the Arab world. At least Gemayel survived his term in office. His successor, Rene Mouawad, was assassinated in 1989, seventeen days after his election.

Bashir Gemayel's project to cement Christian supremacy ended instead with the erosion of Christian power. Maronite factions quarreled among themselves. After having been crippled militarily by Israel's assault, Syria returned to dominate Lebanon.

In 1989, Syria, with backing of the United States and Saudi Arabia, brokered the so-called Taif agreement, which redistributed power in the Lebanese government. Christians held on to a weakened presidency and the post of army chief of staff, but surrendered a majority in parliament, which took on added powers.

Syria was supposed to leave Lebanon within two years after Taif, but didn't. Taif was to pave the way to non-sectarian politics, but also did not. Whole new preoccupations sprung up: Hezbollah, the assertive Shiite militia, matured in the south and in suburbs of Beirut. Besides becoming the leading force in battling Israel, Hezbollah represented Shiite Muslims whose numbers had vastly increased since the National Pact and who were no longer satisfied with being junior players in Lebanon's political stage.

Israel, the erstwhile Maronite patron, got tangled up trying to control far south Lebanon, until it retreated in the year 2000 under persistent military attacks from Hezbollah. Ambushes and roadside bombs sapped Israel's will to stay. Christians were pushed to the sidelines.

"We lost," Amine Gemayel told me in a conversation at his home in June 2015.

Amine lives up in the old Gemayel mountain fiefdom of Bikfaya inland from Beirut. In these mountains, Maronites will tell you, Christians took refuge from marauding Muslims and unlike other Christian communities, refused submission to Islam.

In the eleventh century, the Maronites welcomed the Crusaders when they tried to reconquer the Holy Land and ever since have viewed themselves as a Western outpost, not an appendage of the Arab and Islamic Middle East. France sliced Lebanon from Syria specifically to conserve a Christian enclave.

Despite steady emigration, the Christians, including Orthodox communities and Armenians, managed to hold on and even to prosper, thanks in part to remittances from abroad.

In Amine Gemayel's view, Lebanese Christians have a new mission. It is no longer to dominate Lebanon but to be a bulwark against religious intolerance. "Lebanon has a special vocation, not only for its democratic experience, however imperfect. We want to preserve coexistence," he said, pointing to the country's electoral system and parliament (but leaving out the sectarian violence).

That mission included getting rid of Syrian influence, though both Christian and Maronite factions occasionally enjoyed Syrian sponsorship. To accomplish that goal, a new hero arrived in the person of a Sunni two-time prime minister, billionaire Rafik

Hariri. Gemayel remembers meeting with Hariri representatives, along with other confessional leaders, at Beirut's Bristol Hotel in 2004, and being impressed by his determination to expel Syria from Lebanon.

The Kataeb, down on its luck, cleaved to Hariri's vision. "We could finally be taken out of the Middle East cycle of violence," Amine Gemayel thought.

However, pulling Lebanon out of the Holy Land maelstrom is more easily imagined than done. In the eyes of regional powers, there's no such thing as neutrality. Syria did not take kindly to Hariri's display of independence. In 2005, as a motorcade transporting Hariri motored along Beirut's waterfront, a car bomb exploded and killed him and twenty-one other people. Syria was widely blamed and nine years later, a United Nations investigation continues to probe the blast. Hariri's son, Saad, replaced him as prime minister.

After the Hariri murder, massive protest demonstrations compelled Syria to withdraw its troops from Lebanon. The assassinations nonetheless continued. Another nine politicians and journalists who supported Hariri died in subsequent killings. Among them was Pierre Gemayel Jr., one of Amine's two sons, who seemed poised to return his family to political prominence.

Gemayel was killed when gunmen rammed his car in a Beirut suburb and opened fire. He died on the way to a hospital. Syria expressed dismay, but the Hariri faction blamed Bashar al-Assad.

Meanwhile, Sunni concerns have eclipsed Christian issues. Lebanese Sunnis have become alarmed at recent Shiite ascendancy on several fronts, and not just in Lebanon. First there was the 2003 overthrow of Saddam Hussein and the ushering in of a Shiite-led government in Iraq. Then came Hariri's assassination, possibly carried out by Shiite Iran's Lebanese ally, Hezbollah. Then in 2011, as Syrian Sunnis rose up against Bashar al-Assad, Iran and Hezbollah rushed to his aid.

Amine Gemayel is concerned that the Syrian war could spread into Lebanon, or at least that contagion from the rivalries could renew conflict in his country: Christians in Syria are largely supporting Assad, while Sunnis revile him. Immunization against such an eventuality, he said, requires agreement by Lebanese Christians, Sunnis, and Shiites that the country, at all costs, must avoid getting sucked in.

"We have it pretty good in comparison with the regional turmoil. We have to preserve what we have. As it turns out, Lebanon is a better model for coexistence than the one produced by our neighbors," he said. "From the beginning our model was right."

6/ EGYPT: THE FALSE SPRING

And I will stir up against the Egyptians, and they will fight, each against another and each against his neighbor, city against city, kingdom against kingdom.

—Isaiah 19:2

On January 6, 2012—Christmas Eve on the Eastern Christian calendar—Pope Shenouda III, spiritual leader of Egypt's seven million Coptic Orthodox Christians, was greeting the country's military rulers at Midnight Mass in Cairo's St. Mark's Cathedral. He wore gold-trimmed vestments and sported an abundant gray beard. The army officers sat stiff-backed in the front pew, clad in olive dress uniforms and emotionless faces.

For as long as anyone could remember, this holiday tableau was a tradition. But in the eyes of Bishoy Tamry, a young Coptic political activist who was watching from the rear, this was no time for the old-fashioned niceties. Just three months before, on October 9, 2011, soldiers posted at Maspero, the state television and information headquarters in Cairo, had killed two dozen peaceful Coptic demonstrators. A pair of armored personnel carriers driven by soldiers who had run amok crushed at least thirteen people. The rest of the victims were shot dead.

Bishoy had been at Maspero. His friend and fellow protestor, Mina Daniel, was gunned down as the pair fled the mayhem. Both had taken part in the 2011 struggle in Tahrir Square to topple dictator Hosni Mubarak and rallied young Copts to stand up for their rights. Daniel was especially charismatic and had campaigned to reduce hostility between Muslims and Christians. He was shot in the chest and ended up dead in a refrigerated morgue at Coptic Hospital.

And now Pope Shenouda, in the quavering voice of old age, welcomed Daniel's executioners. Among them sat General Hamdy Badeen, commander of the military police that had gone on the rampage.

Bishoy and two comrades couldn't contain themselves. "They killed our brothers! They killed your children!" they shouted. A pair of brawny congregants hustled the threesome outside.

The scene startled the congregation. Not only had the youths confronted the all-powerful military, but they had interrupted the pope, incontrovertible leader of the Coptic community. And it had all been broadcast live across Egypt on TV! As far as Bishoy was concerned, that was the point: to announce far and wide that the dictatorship was evil and that the hierarchy was wrong to cozy up to it.

Criticism of church leaders was a highly unusual step. Christian minorities had been taught from childhood to let clerics handle dealings with authority. For Copts, the pope was the supreme community representative. He would manage sectarian disputes and relations with the government.

To Bishoy, this old survival strategy outlived its usefulness. In the first decade of the twenty-first century, thousands of young Coptic activists decided that clerical bowing and scraping had brought Copts only discrimination and humiliation. A new Egypt was required.

Bishoy Tamry's saga is the story of Egyptian Copts' attempt to free themselves from dictatorship, second-class citizenship, and sectarian tensions that characterize the entire Holy Land. It was also an effort to take their fate into their own hands. These endeavors were exhilarating at first, and then, along with Egypt's democratic aspirations, they collapsed.

Coptic youth participation in Tahrir Square was a fragment of the Arab Spring mosaic. Youth across the Middle East—Christian, Muslim, and non-believer alike—looked to upend autocratic rule. In late 2010 and early 2011, young people rose up in Tunisia to overthrow long-time dictator President Zine el-Abidine Ben Ali. His downfall was the starting gun for uprisings elsewhere. In Syria, similar efforts were met with brutal gunfire that transformed a peaceful revolt into a bloody civil war. In Libya, rebels with the aid of NATO airpower toppled Moammar Gadaffi only to unleash an anarchic multi-sided civil conflict.

In Egypt, tens of thousands gathered in Cairo and other cities to bring an end to the thirty-year rule of President Hosni Mubarak. For Egypt's Christian youth, the uprising against autocratic rule was at the same time a rebellion against church leaders, whom they viewed as complicit in the community's chronic subjugation. They threw in their lot with the concept of full and equal citizenship for all. Their establishment elders warned it would be risky. Who knew what would come from change?

The massacre at Maspero, ten months after Mubarak's ouster, was an early sign of failure. The post-Mubarak government communicated that little had changed in Egypt. Afterwards, crackdowns on political protests grew more frequent.

Police and soldiers stood by and did nothing as churches came under assault by mobs of Muslim fanatics. Characteristically, the church hierarchy passively accepted the violence and, worse, bowed to the new order.

So on that Christmas Eve, Bishoy decided to fight on. "If I couldn't get justice for the dead at Maspero, what justice can we get?" he asked himself. "I owed it to Mina. I owed it to all the martyrs."

Bishoy Tamry's revolt, like those of other young Egyptians, was years in the making. He was twenty-three years old at the time of the Christmas Eve outburst but was already an experienced organizer. He belonged to the Maspero Youth Union, a civil rights organization that took its name from a demonstration at the television headquarters a few months before the October massacre. It, too, had been broken up by police and local vigilantes.

For a boy from the sleepy provinces of Egypt, activism had been a bold departure. The pint-sized computer geek with a scraggly beard grew up in the southern Egyptian town of Nag Hammadi along the Nile River. Houses there are set among date palms. Grain and sugar cane fields surround the town. Donkeys compete with motorized rickshaws on dusty, unpaved streets. Muslims sometimes mark their homes with paintings of the Kaaba, the sacred stone in Mecca. Christians put images of St. George over their front doors. It's an out-of-the-way place where rhythms are slow and the main escape for restless young people is to go to Cairo for school or work.

Bishoy learned early that Christians were considered inferior by many Muslims and the government. State schools held separate religion classes for Muslims and Christians. The Muslims got their lessons in a room, the Copts in a courtyard. A teacher remarked to Bishoy that if he attended lectures on Islam he would learn "good things." Government television broadcast rivers of Islamic sermons but never Christian ones.

"I laughed it off. Life being second class was just kind of normal," he said.

A sectarian earthquake shook Bishoy out of lethargy. On Coptic Christmas Eve, January 6, 2010, three Muslim gunmen ambushed worshippers as they left services at St. Mary's Church in Nag Hammadi. Six Copts died, along with a Muslim who happened to be riding in a car with Christian friends. Instead of returning home to a joyful Christmas meal, Copts found themselves fleeing bullets and navigating the streets through puddles of blood.

Wild rumors of possible motives circulated. Maybe the killing was in revenge for the local clergy's refusal to support a parliamentary candidate from Mubarak's ruling party. Maybe it had to do with unrest in the nearby hamlet of Farsut, where a Copt was accused of sexually abusing a Muslim girl. Or maybe it was a spin-off from another nearby riot in which Muslims violently objected to the presence of a church.

No matter. Bishoy noted a pair of disturbing reactions: police stationed near St. Mary's failed to guard the church, even though the local bishop had informed them of threats; and church officials muted their outrage after the incident. When youths in Nag Hammadi mounted a protest demonstration, the town bishop told them to go home.

"It was the first time I saw that the church was not protecting the flock. It was time to move outside the church walls," Bishoy said.

He joined a nationwide youth group called Copts for Egypt, which had grown out of another organization, Egyptians Against Religious Discrimination. The latter group was founded in 2006 in response to yet another atrocity: knife attacks at four churches in Alexandria on Coptic worshippers by three Muslim men. Christians took to the streets in protest and got into fistfights with Muslims. Church officials quickly moved to tamp down the anger. Father Augustinos, a Coptic priest, told the demonstrators, "To protest doesn't do any good for the country." In tandem, the Mubarak government trotted out an all-purpose explanation for such attacks: the assailants were crazy.

Coptic youth weren't buying it. The problem was not just ever-present sectarian tensions. It was a problem of a dictatorship that tolerated such violence.

This defiant attitude did not emerge in a vacuum. In early twenty-first-century Egypt, all sorts of organized protest groups were forming. Political and social communication aided by the Internet exploded. In 2003, demonstrations against government policy toward the Palestinian–Israeli conflict morphed into calls for political change. Several private newspapers began to criticize rich-get-richer economic policies. Social activists used mobile phone video cameras to broadcast what state TV would not: scenes of police torture and beatings. Voters resisted election fraud by storming the polls.

Small, but bold, dissident groups took to the streets to denounce authoritarian rule. One group in particular, called Kifaya, inspired Coptic youth. Kifaya means "enough" in Arabic. It spearheaded demonstrations in central Cairo, where usually riot police far outnumbered the marchers.

Kifaya was led by leftist activist George Ishak, a Copt. He and representatives of old-line opposition groups got together in a variety of dingy Cairo downtown offices to plot Mubarak's downfall. Some were socialists, some were nationalists. Others were leftover communists, and the rest members of Islamist groups— including the Muslim Brotherhood, Egypt's largest dissident organization.

The fact that a Christian led Kifaya entranced Bishoy Tamry. "This was important," he said. "George Ishak was both a Christian and a leader. I hadn't seen anything like that. We Copts aren't supposed to complain, much less be out front. George Ishak showed that even we could lead."

Across the country, demonstrations grew large and labor unrest spread. On November 24, 2010, the Coptic Youth Front confronted the authorities in a novel way.

Police had gathered to attack Cairo's St. Mary's church, a hulking brick structure on the west side of the Nile. Copts had been building an annex to it when the governor of Giza suddenly decided that the activity broke construction codes. Copts "were in the process of building a dome, which indicates their intention to turn the center into a church," he announced, even though the locale was already a church. It was a convenient justification for the governor because in Egypt, Christians needed presidential permission to build a church.

Workers and congregants resisted police by throwing rocks. Police responded with tear gas and by tossing stones off a nearby overpass. They eventually used firearms. One Coptic defender was shot and killed inside the church. Bishoy gathered activists together. They marched up a main street to the Giza district governor's office, and shouted "Down with Mubarak" and "The government is extremist." Broadcast on TV, the incident exposed a broad audience to a rare sight: a crowd calling for Mubarak's ouster and police unable to stop them.

Horrified church leaders apologized to the government. After objections from the youth, Pope Shenouda complained to the government that "Coptic blood is not cheap." It would have been a victory of sorts except that 120 Coptic protestors were kept in detention for several weeks. State television labeled them thugs. The Coptic Youth Union went into hiding.

Union members emerged five weeks later to protest a fearful act of anti-Christian terror. During New Year's services at Two Saints Church in Alexandra, a suicide car bomb killed twenty-four people and wounded eighty others. Parked cars exploded in flames and blood splashed the church walls. Street fighting broke out between enraged Copts and Muslims. Police beat any Christian they found. The Mubarak government announced that the Alexandria perpetrator was a single suicide bomber on foot and suggested that the killer was—what else? —crazy.

In Cairo, the Coptic Youth Union organized a protest. The group accused the government of ignoring the obvious: that such an attack was clearly organized and a symptom of wider dangers to Christians. In Cairo, demonstrators marched from the mixed-Christian–Muslim neighborhood of Shoubra to St. Mark's Cathedral, seat of the Coptic Orthodox Church. There, they clashed with police and returned to Shoubra for a sit-in. Muslim sympathizers joined and helped lead chants against the government.

Once again, church leaders were dismayed. A priest helped police single out Muslims for arrest. Bishoy scolded the cleric, "You know nothing. These people are here to express sympathy with us."

The Shoubra march and sit-in turned out to be merely a warm-up. Less than a month later, on January 25, 2011, democracy activists took over Tahrir Square for a massive anti-government demonstration.

Tahrir Square is less a plaza than a slow moving merry-go-round of massive traffic jams. Framed by icons of Egypt's ancient and modern history, it is a fitting arena for revolt.

On the north side stands the Egyptian Museum, Cairo's antiquated showcase of mummies and treasures. On the east side, apartment buildings constructed in French architectural style exemplify the country's nineteenth-century efforts to Westernize. To the south looms the Mugamma, a giant grey bureaucratic building constructed under Egypt's last monarch. It was meant to efficiently deliver state services in one locale to all. Seventy years on, it is a nightmarish symbol of government ineptitude, a chaotic, dingy place where citizens hire guides to lead them from office to office to deal with (and pay bribes to) indifferent bureaucrats.

Next to the Mugamma stands the Omar Makram Mosque, named after a preacher who campaigned for independence from the Ottoman Empire and also resisted Napoleon's 1798 invasion of Egypt. Anchoring the southwest part of the square are headquarters of the Arab League, created by Gamal Abdul Nasser to highlight the country's regional leadership. Next door is the former Nile Hilton Hotel, the city's first international-style glass building and a twentieth-century symbol of surface modernity. Finally, just to the north stands the burnt-out headquarters of the National Democratic Party, Mubarak's vote-mobilization and patronage machine. Mobs torched it during the Tahrir Square upheaval.

On January 25, 2011, Tahrir hosted the biggest sit-in in Egyptian history. All the streams of opposition gathered. Middle class bloggers were joined by newly independent workers' unions, women's groups, and old-line dissidents. The Muslim Brotherhood, which at first opposed the protest, showed up on January 28.

Most significantly, in poured a vast population of unemployed and underemployed youth, who had plenty of time on their hands and resentment to match.

Pope Shenouda told Christians to stay away. They came anyway.

The Coptic Youth Union set up two tents and marched under a banner adorned with the cross and crescent—an emblem of the 1919 uprising against Great Britain. It was a brief, shining moment. Muslims and Christians found common ground in a search for a new Egypt. A Coptic choir named after the Legion of Thebes, a group of Christian martyred during the Roman Empire, sang on a stage. In case of police attack, Christians formed a cordon around Muslims when they held Friday prayers in the square and Muslims returned the favor during Sunday Mass.

State media insulted the protestors and put out word that foreigners were paying Bishoy and his colleagues to destabilize Egypt. Back in Nag Hammadi, Bishoy's parents became alarmed and his father rifled through his bedroom looking for suspicious cash. "He didn't find any and told me, 'Okay, you are free to keep protesting,'" Bishoy recalled.

Coptic kids camped out in the square or commuted to and from crammed apartments around town. They chanted by day and sang by night. They fashioned a cardboard obelisk bearing the names of demonstrators who had been slain. On January 28, police responded by killing hundreds of protestors and arresting supporters in and outside the square. Still the throng did not disperse. Bishoy scoured pharmacies for medicines and bakeries for bread to supply the protestors.

On February 11, 2011, a junta of generals ousted Mubarak from power. The announcement was made on television by General Omar Suleiman, the aging intelligence chief. He said that the president had ceded power to the Supreme Council of the Armed Forces, a collection of officers that would oversee a transition to democracy. Mubarak was flown from Cairo by helicopter to Sharm el-Sheikh, the Red Sea resort where he had a palace.

The Tahrir crowd erupted in cheers. Egyptian flags waved in the square from end to end. Dancing broke out in the Coptic Youth Union tents. "We didn't really think about what the future would hold. We thought our mission was accomplished," Bishoy said. The Coptic Youth Union disbanded.

Buyer's remorse soon became a chronic condition among Egyptian democracy activists. The joy that greeted the dictator's removal turned to disappointment. Mubarak's military successors repeatedly attacked demonstrators in and around Tahrir Square. Dozens were killed.

Egypt's economy nosedived. Crime and chaos spread across the country as police retired from the streets. Political infighting tore at the unity of Tahrir Square: Muslims organized their own demonstrations, excluding Copts; conservative Muslims excluded liberal Muslims; women were assaulted by thugs. Nearby merchants grew resentful of the clogging of downtown traffic.

Copts felt the chill early. On February 21, just eleven days after Mubarak fell, soldiers bulldozed a wall surrounding the St. Bishoy monastery, a desert complex built in the fifth century. The wall had been constructed to keep marauders out during the weeks of Tahrir chaos. Armored personnel carriers knocked down a ceremonial front gate. Soldiers used rocket-propelled grenades and rifle fire to disperse monks. The Supreme Council of the Armed Forces claimed the wall stood illegally on state land.

The news hit Bishoy hard. Not only were Mubarak's cronies still in charge, they were as bullying as ever. The Coptic Youth Union, so quickly demobilized after Mubarak's fall, reunited.

The Union would soon have plenty to protest. Salafi-led jihad was taking hold in Egypt. The authorities did nothing to stop it. In March, after rumors that a Christian man had had an affair with a Muslim woman, a Muslim mob assaulted the Church of Two Martyrs in the town of Atfih, ten miles south of Cairo. The crowd broke through church walls with sledgehammers and set chairs on fire inside. Coptic lawyers presented a list of one hundred identified intruders. Public prosecutors neither interviewed nor prosecuted anyone. The government repaired the church.

Four days after the Atfih vandalism, Christians held a protest march in Muqattam, a suburb on Cairo's eastern outskirts. A dispute over blocked traffic ignited a street fight that gave way to the looting of Coptic homes and businesses. Thirteen people died in the violence. A priest and a group of Coptic residents trapped a dozen looters and handed them over to police. Lawyers presented the names of the suspects to the public prosecutor. No one was ever charged.

A week later, in the southern Egyptian town of Qena, Salafi Muslims cut off the ear of a Coptic schoolteacher and threw him off a second story balcony. They said he was running a prostitution ring. He reported the attack to police, but no one was arrested.

In May, a Muslim mob stormed a pair of churches in Embaba, a Cairo slum on the Nile's west bank. Rioters believed that a Coptic woman who had converted to Islam was being detained against her will in one of the churches. She wasn't, but that didn't stop the riots. Mobs set fire to each church.

Bishoy went to Embaba to record the damage. "Some thieves were trapped on the third floor of a building while other rioters were setting the first floor on fire. The looters leapt out of windows to escape," he recalled. "It would be funny, if it wasn't so tragic."

Police neither showed up at the churches nor at any of the looted homes or businesses. They informed panicked Copts they had orders not to "engage" the mob.

In response, the Coptic Youth Union returned to the streets. Dozens of members held an eleven-day sit-in at the Maspero state television building. They accused government TV of distorting reports of attacks on Christians and blaming the Copts. The protestors demanded that police arrest the perpetrators of the Embaba violence, repair the churches and establish a government hotline to report incidents. The government agreed to both the hotline and the repairs, but not the arrests.

In July, Bishoy and the Union returned to Maspero after a fresh anti-Christian riot in the northern Cairo suburb of Ain Shams. Ain Shams is a conservative Muslim and Salafi stronghold. A year earlier, Christians had renovated a disused underwear factory for conversion into a church. A mob marched on the building, chanted "God is great," and shuttered it.

The Coptic Youth Union called for both the opening of the church and the ouster of the post-Mubarak military regime. "They had done nothing about Embaba or Ain Shams," said Bishoy. "So nothing had changed."

The military resorted to an old Mubarak-era tactic. Soldiers recruited local residents who were upset over disruption of traffic to attack the sit-in at Maspero. The mob used sticks and knives while police looked on. The Copts dispersed and, to memorialize the break-up, changed the group's name to Maspero Youth Union.

On October 4, Maspero Youth Union reconvened at the television building. This time it was to protest an attack on St. George's church in the distant southern village of Marinab, in Aswan province. Muslim residents, led by a Salafi preacher, had torched St. George's on the grounds that its domes were too big. The vandals also found time to run off with a refrigerator, a television, and money from the donations box. Aswan's governor blamed the Christians.

Maspero Youth demanded that the governor be fired. The central government declined. State media quickly said Christians caused the problem. A Muslim preacher said the Copts' actions had humiliated an "Islamic ruler of a Muslim nation."

Soldiers and police attacked the October 4 protestors. As the demonstrators scattered, a group of eight soldiers pounced on a young man and beat him with sticks and batons. Police and plain-clothes agents joined in and dragged the youth away. A hidden video cam captured the attack and it went viral on YouTube.

Undeterred, Maspero Youth Union and other Coptic groups prepared for a massive march on October 9. It would be a tragic turning point not only for the Coptic activists, but for Egypt's Arab Spring.

Even before the October 9 Maspero massacre, attacks on post-Mubarak demonstrations by the army and police were occurring with increasing frequency. All summer and into the fall, groups re-occupied Tahrir Square, called for an end to military rule and tried to march on Interior Ministry headquarters.

Time and again, security forces rushed the square, beat pro-testors and tore down their tents, sometimes setting them on fire. The demonstrators were led by hard-core soccer fans who often clashed with police at stadiums. They stormed giant concrete barricades that blocked police headquarters and threw rocks. Snipers responded by aiming at the eyes of individual demonstrators as well as at journalists.

The October 9 attack on Coptic protestors at Maspero was the bloodiest crackdown yet and made clear that Egypt's new rulers would tolerate no more Tahrir-style protests.

The march began in Shoubra, a relatively leafy suburb on Cairo's north side. Shoubra houses several churches, and residents took pride in Muslim-Christian coexistence.

At 4 p.m., thousands of demonstrators gathered, including Muslim sympathizers. The mood was festive at first, but the atmosphere soon soured. As the stream of protestors, many carrying large crosses, neared downtown, residents and bystanders pelted them with stones. Many Cairenes were fed up with demonstrations. State television accused the Copts of fomenting sectarian violence.

The march flowed toward the train station and then down a wide boulevard to the Nile River near the Ramses Hilton Hotel. There it turned north toward Maspero. Soldiers stood guard at the entrance of the curved building. The crowd pressed against a metal barricade out front.

Shots rang out. Demonstrators scattered toward the Hilton and into an open-air bus station nearby. It was already dark.

Suddenly an armored personnel carrier careened from Maspero toward them. And then another, weaving down the road as if to hit as many people as possible.

Someone's head was crushed under a tire. Another two protestors were smashed against a ramp leading up to a Nile bridge. A soldier atop an APC fired his AK-47 at people who were pressed against a railing along the riverbank. Frantic demonstrators fought back with sticks, fruitlessly banging them against the armored cars. One youth hurled a large chunk of concrete into an open hatch on one of the vehicles.

Bishoy was there along with his friend Mina Daniel, twenty years old at the time. Daniel's family, like Bishoy's, hailed from southern Egypt, but had moved to Cairo in the early 1990s to flee suffocating sectarian tensions. He, like Bishoy, turned to protest politics after the Nag Hammadi killings. A lithe figure with a tangled Che Guevara beard, Daniel was a popular leader. In Tahrir, he had made a point of singing revolutionary songs and mingling with Muslims. Back in January, the police shot him in the leg, but he stayed in the square to promote democracy and preach tolerance. Now, as he and Bishoy fled a fast approaching APC, Daniel fell. Bishoy and others hauled him to an ambulance.

Bishoy didn't notice the blood spreading on Daniel's chest.

Bishoy took refuge inside an office building. Several dead bodies and more wounded lay on the floor. He ran outside and mounted the back of someone's motorcycle to get to Coptic Hospital, a couple of miles away. Along the journey, a reporter phoned and asked if any soldiers had been killed, as state television was reporting. Bishoy answered, "The army is not the martyr here. The army is the enemy of Egypt."

Unknown to Bishoy, a news reader on government TV had invited "honest Egyptians" to take to the streets and defend the soldiers. Residents pursued the demonstrators with sticks and swords.

Inside Coptic Hospital, some corpses lined the floor and others were stored inside refrigerated cabinets. Some of the bodies were mangled, the result of being run over or dragged by armored military vehicles. Others were shot, some in the head. Relatives tip-toed around the clusters of bodies. Someone told Bishoy that his friend was there, "the one with the long hair and beard." It was Daniel, dead. "I blanked out," Bishoy recalled, his voice faltering.

A priest tried to persuade relatives to quickly take bodies of their loved ones to the cathedral for the pope's blessing. Bishoy opposed the request and said the families ought to let doctors perform autopsies. That way, the cause of death would be known and perhaps responsibility fixed.

"It's enough," the priest said.

"This is our blood, but you don't value it," Bishoy responded.

"The government will oppose this. The Muslims have gathered outside," the priest implored. On the street in front of the hospital, a mob called the Christians "dogs," "Jews," enemies of Islam, and enemies of Egypt.

"Then we will die here," Bishoy said.

Families, among them relatives of Daniel, agreed to the autopsies. Eight victims died of bullet wounds, two of blows to the head and one from slashes by knife or sword. Thirteen others had been crushed by the armored vehicles. "This was no longer about being Copts and being able to pray. It was not even just about the January revolution. It was about the right to live on this land," said Bishoy.

It took three days for Pope Shenouda to respond to the killings. He called the victims martyrs and rejected the charge that Copts had attacked soldiers. But he also dismissed demands from victims' families for an international investigation. Shenouda said the call would harm the "national unity that we are all defending."

After the Maspero killings, lethal attacks on demonstrators multiplied. In late November, police shot down about fifty anti-army demonstrators on Mohammed Mahmoud Street, just off Tahrir Square.

In Port Said on February 2, 2012, police let fans of the home team assault followers of Cairo's Ahly, the country's most successful soccer team, inside the stadium. Ahly fans had spear-headed several Tahrir demonstrations. Someone mysteriously locked exit doors in the stadium and turned out the lights. Seventy Ahly fans died, as police stood aside.

The unity that had helped bring down Mubarak fully broke down. The Muslim Brotherhood and other conservative Islamic parties sided with the army over the Maspero massacre. Attacks on Copts increased. Muslims expelled an extended Coptic family from a suburb of Alexandria on the basis of rumors that the phone belonging to one of its members contained compromising photos of a Muslim woman. Looting of homes and businesses accompanied the expulsion. Police declined to intervene, except to hold a town meeting to ratify the eviction. From one end of Egypt to the other, Copts were arrested for offending Islam under rules that made it a crime to "insult" religion.

In Cairo, graffiti artists painted portraits of a smiling Mina Daniel on walls near Tahrir Square and other parts of downtown. Bishoy's friend had become the icon of a fading dream.

On March 17, 2012, Shenouda III, the 117th patriarch of the Coptic Orthodox Church, Pope of Alexandria, and Patriarch of all Africa on the Holy Throne of Saint Mark the Evangelist and Holy

Apostle, died at the age of eighty-eight. He had been the spiritual leader of the Coptic community for forty years.

Shenouda's death coincided with a new phase in post-Mubarak turbulence: the ascent to power of the Muslim Brotherhood. The Brotherhood was Egypt's oldest, largest, and best organized opposition group. Its membership was estimated a million strong. By the time of Shenouda's death, the Brotherhood had already won parliamentary elections and was set to field a candidate in the 2012 presidential election. Together with a Salafi party, Islamist groups controlled more than two-thirds of the new legislature.

In June 2012, the candidate for the Brotherhood's Freedom and Justice Party, Mohamed Morsi, was elected president. The legislature fashioned a new constitution that designated Islam as a main source of legislation and tasked clerics from al-Azhar, a complex of Islamic schools of higher education, to ensure that legal statutes accorded with Islamic law.

For older Copts, it was a bittersweet I-told-you-so moment. Church officials who had warned against revolt were being proven right. Under democracy, things would get worse for Christians.

On July 26, 2012, shortly after Morsi's election, a Christian laundry owner in the village of Dashur singed a shirt belonging to a Muslim customer. The aggrieved customer returned to the laundry with hundreds of cohorts carrying swords and knives. Christians defended their homes with fire bombs.

A Muslim died of third-degree burns. One hundred twenty Coptic families fled the village. During the entire five-day melee, police refused to intervene. Morsi, much in line with previous governments, dismissed the incident as isolated. No one was arrested for the sacking of Christian homes. Three Copts were jailed and charged with possessing explosives.

Next April, in the village of Khusus near Cairo, a dispute over the alleged harassment of a Coptic woman by a Muslim man turned violent. A Salafi preacher accused Coptic children of drawing a swastika on a mosque wall. Muslims burned Christian homes, vehicles, and shops. By nightfall, five Copts had been shot dead. Police stood by without moving.

Two days later, in Cairo, Muslim civilians and police besieged St. Mark's Cathedral during funerals for the Khusus dead. They pelted the church with rocks and bottles and then fired shots at the building. Mourners inside shouted "Down with Morsi." Police tossed tear gas onto church grounds even as plainclothes gunmen fired on the Christians. Two Coptic mourners died.

Morsi promised an investigation, but nothing came of it. Pope Tawadros II, Shenouda's successor, rebuked the president. "The Egyptian church has never been subjected to this, even in the worst ages," he said.

Opposition to Morsi grew all over Egypt. The president managed to offend millions of Muslim Egyptians, many of whom felt he had become a dictator. In November 2012, Morsi decreed his decisions immune from judicial review. In a stroke, he became the supreme law of the land. Demonstrations against him mounted and, across Egypt, physical attacks on Morsi's Freedom and Justice Party offices broke out.

A big demonstration at the presidential Ettihadiya Palace in Heliopolis took place on December 4, 2012. The Maspero Youth Union took part and set up its tent. It looked like another Tahrir was in the making.

Morsi struck back. Under the impassive gaze of riot police, hundreds of Muslim Brotherhood members and supporters assaulted the demonstrators at the presidential palace. They broke up the sit-in, tore down tents, and ransacked the possessions of anti-Morsi protestors.

Over the next twelve hours, violence between pro- and anti-Morsi mobs escalated into exchanges of rifle and gunfire and Molotov cocktails. Neither the Central Security Forces—Egypt's riot police—nor the Ettihadiya presidential guard nor the military police made an effort to halt the violence. Civil war seemed imminent.

On the evening of December 5, Essam al-Erian, deputy secretary of the Brotherhood's Freedom and Justice Party, appeared on live television and declared that "Everyone must go now to Ettihadiya and surround the thugs. . . . Then we can arrest them all." Other Brotherhood members issued similar calls over social media. Morsi supporters nabbed forty-nine protestors near Ettihadiya palace, hauled them to the front gate, and beat them.

Bishoy Tamry was there and watched as a friend was kicked and punched. He himself escaped during a momentary lull in the abductions. "I knew then, Morsi simply had to go," Bishoy said.

Over the next six months, pressure on Morsi increased. A group of activists in an organization called Tamarod, or Rebel, drew up a petition to demand his ouster. Millions signed. Tamarod and other anti-Morsi groups called for a demonstration in Tahrir on June 30, 2013.

Once again, Maspero Youth Union took to the square. Army chief Abdel Fattah al-Sisi appealed to the crowd for instructions on what to do. Sisi had taken over the reins of the army after the previous junta gave up power to Morsi. Relatively young at age fifty-nine, Sisi spoke of democratic transition and stability. Egyptians craved the latter.

Sisi's genius was persuading masses of Egyptians to give him free reign to depose Morsi by any means he saw fit. On July 1, Sisi told Morsi to leave power voluntarily or be kicked out. "If you have not obeyed the people after forty-eight hours, it will be our duty to put forward a road map for the future instead," he warned.

On July 3, Sisi announced the dismissal and arrest of Morsi and his replacement by the constitutional court chief. He closed down Islamist TV stations and rounded up hundreds of Brotherhood officials and supporters. The military presented itself as savior of the nation.

For Christians, it was back to the future. Once again, the pope became the supreme intermediary between the Coptic community and the authorities. Pope Tawadros literally stood shoulder to shoulder with the new military strongman: when Sisi made his televised announcement deposing Morsi, Tawadros, along with the chief al-Azhar preacher, flanked him on the stage.

Dancing broke out in the Coptic tent in Tahrir, just as it had two and a half years before. But this time, Bishoy didn't celebrate. He stood quietly in a corner. A friend came up to ask what was up.

"Is something troubling you?"

"I don't know. I think we should wait to see what happens," Bishoy answered.

On walls near Tahrir, municipal workers stripped off portraits commemorating revolutionary martyrs, including those of Mina Daniel. Posters of Sisi, sometimes accompanied by photos of Gamal Abdul Nasser and Anwar Sadat, were pasted up in their place.

Christians suffered an immediate Islamist backlash over Morsi's downfall. Perhaps it was simply easier for Morsi supporters to focus their frustration on the vulnerable Copts, a 10 per cent minority in the country, than to take on the far more numerous Muslims who also had wanted Morsi gone.

The Brotherhood's website said that the Copts' "satanic propaganda machine" had mobilized Egyptians against Morsi. Members of the Maspero Youth Union were labeled "those who killed soldiers" and accused the group of being the vanguard of anti-Morsi petitioners.

The speed, frequency, and intensity of mob violence against Copts was without precedent in modern Egyptian history. In Marsa Matrouh on the Mediterranean coast, a mob burned a security guard post at St. Mary's Church. On July 5 in Nag Hassan, near Luxor, rumors that Christians had drowned a Muslim man in the Nile provoked riots that ended with four Copts beaten to death and several others injured. A police officer told Human Rights Watch that there was no use in trying to stop these incidents because "people are stupid." Two dozen Coptic homes were damaged or destroyed.

In Sinai, between July 5 and 11, two Coptic lay people were beheaded and a Coptic priest was shot to death.

In Delga, a small town near Minya in southern Egypt, Morsi supporters looted and torched two churches. Others tried to burn a church in Qena, but, unusually, police stopped them by firing tear gas.

Bishoy responded philosophically to the wall-to-wall assaults. "It was the price we paid for getting rid of Islamic extremists," he said.

In the meantime, Sisi was being hailed as Egypt's new redeemer. Copts were big supporters. Although a new constitution reaffirmed Islam as a main source of legislation, it left interpretation of law in the hands of civil courts rather than al-Azhar. The process for permitting Church construction would be eased.

Bishoy and other of the more liberal Coptic activists grew wary. Egypt's fate was once again in the hands of a military government—even as police and the army did little to inhibit the anti-Copt attacks.

On August 14, 2013, Sisi ordered the removal of thousands of pro-Morsi demonstrators from Rabaa Square, which is located in a high-rise Cairo neighborhood on the way to the airport. The onslaught against protestors across Egypt was bloodier even than Mubarak's January 2011 crackdowns. At least eight hundred people died in one day, almost all of them unarmed protestors. Sisi justified the violence in the name of anti-terrorism.

Bishoy was stunned. He himself had visited Rabaa and found it peaceful. Now, the expulsion elevated Brotherhood members to martyrdom and soaked Egypt's promised road to democracy in blood. "Sisi justified the complaints of the Brotherhood. He should have let the protests go on," Bishoy said.

Yet many Copts were overjoyed at the crackdown. On October 9, 2013, Coptic groups held a second anniversary candlelight commemoration of the Maspero killings. It was a bittersweet and strange affair. On the one hand, the protestors were demanding justice for the Coptic dead—which meant putting high-ranking army officers on trial. On the other hand, Copts, including some from the Maspero Youth Union, praised the army for crushing the Muslim Brotherhood at Rabaa Square with a death toll that dwarfed Maspero.

This paradox required verbal acrobatics. In a newspaper interview, Bishoy tried to square the circle: "We can't hold the entire army responsible for what happened at Rabaa," he said.

The Maspero Youth Union endorsed the new constitution, even though it solidified the army's hold on power, reaffirmed the army's power to try civilians in military courts, and gave the hated Interior Ministry a veto over legislative police reform measures.

Bishoy and a minority of other Maspero Youth dissented. The goal of democracy had been smashed, they argued. Moreover, mass arrests were not just aimed at the Brotherhood's so-called network of terrorists, but at anyone who opposed the new regime.

These included Arab Spring revolutionaries who had stood with the Copts at Maspero.

In January 2014, Egyptians went to the polls to ratify a new constitution. During the day, Bishoy received a phone call from a friend who suggested he leave Cairo because police were rounding up people opposed to the new constitution. By phone from Nag Hammadi, Bishoy's parents asked whether it was not time to resume his studies and leave politics behind for a while. Bishoy told them he would see.

But Bishoy was determined to stay. "Otherwise, what were we fighting for? It wasn't just for the Copts and a few churches. We have to keep going."

A few days before the vote, on January 6, 2014, a written Christmas greeting from Sisi was read out at Midnight Mass in St. Mark's Cathedral. It received a long round of applause from the congregants, more lavish even than the clapping when Pope Tawadros appeared at the altar. Bishoy did not attend the service.

7/ PALESTINE AND ISRAEL: CHRISTIANS ADRIFT

It is a sight I shall never forget. Thousands of human beings expelled from their homes, running, crying, shouting in terror. After seeing such a thing, you cannot but become a revolutionary.

—George Habash

On the surface, Christians who live in the occupied Palestinian territories—the West Bank and Gaza Strip—have little in common with those who live inside Israel.

Christians in the Palestinian Territories, numbering around 50,000, are beset by restrictions on travel and commerce. Israeli military occupation frames their lives. They are subject to delays and chronic humiliations at checkpoints and in some cases, forbidden from visiting Jerusalem and its holy sites or anywhere else outside their town of residence. They belong to no universally recognized state. Their population is shrinking.

Christians in Israel, about 163,000, by contrast enjoy freedom of movement and religion and can speak out politically. They live in a growing economy and a sprightly democracy, though they face overt discrimination as Arabs and therefore supposedly alien to the Jewish state. Their passports are recognized internationally, except in most of the Arab world. Their population is growing.

Yet, Christians share a common unease on both sides of the Green Line—the line of demarcation set in 1949 following the 1948 war that brought Israelis statehood and reduced Palestinians to subjection and statelessness. Both communities are experiencing ever more complex identity crises that make them question their attachment to their homeland. In the case of Palestinians in the territories, alienation from the national movement has become a morale-sapper and a major factor in deciding whether to stay in their homeland or emigrate.

Identity problems for West Bank and Gaza Strip Christians may seem odd, given their history. Common identity as a Palestinian has been a point of pride for Christians as well as Muslims since the first inklings of nationalism emerged in the 19th and early 20th centuries. The issue of Christians as a religious minority was a secondary consideration; there were no hyphenated Palestinians. The problem now is that their preferred Palestinian identity is being challenged from within Palestinian society itself.

A rising tide of fundamentalism has been spearheaded by Hamas, the Islamic Resistance Movement, which rules the Gaza Strip and designates Palestine Muslim land in which Christians ought to live under Islamic law. For Christians, this promises second-class citizenship at best.

Christians' national identity is also strained by changes in the posture of the Palestine Liberation Organization (PLO), to which Christian Palestinians have historically been loyal. The PLO's dominant Fatah party, which rules the West Bank, is nominally a secular nationalist organization. Under pressure from Hamas, however, Fatah has increasingly framed the Palestinian struggle for self-determination in Islamic terms.

The Palestinian struggle's turn toward Islamist politics was bound to upset Christians. Christian Palestinians (and most Muslims) have not fought for a state under Islamic law. For Christians, the possible contagion of sectarian conflict from Iraq and Syria into Palestine is also worrisome.

These concerns are largely muted in public. Anyone who broaches the subject is branded an Israeli propagandist who is trying to divide the Palestinians. Suggestions that segments of the Muslim population have become hostile to Christians are scorned. Similar disapproval meets insinuations that Fatah has gradually marginalized Christians from Palestinian politics. We are all Palestinians, the deniers insist.

In a recently published interview, Greek Orthodox archbishop Attalah Hanna adhered to this official script: "We don't divide the Palestinian people based on who is Christian and who is Muslim, who is religious and who isn't, who is left or what party they are a member of. We don't divide the people based on convictions and religion."

Perhaps not, but Christians are talking about it in private if not in public. In Christian enclaves—Bethlehem, Jerusalem, Nablus, Ramallah, el-Bireh—conversations about the Islamist threat can be heard frequently in kitchens and over coffee. The concerns add to traditional motivations for Christian emigration over the years: continued Israeli control over the West Bank and Gaza Strip, the lagging economy, restrictions on travel and the ever-present possibility of war breaking out. Numbers are difficult to estimate, largely due to Palestinian concern that it would harm national morale.

"The emigration phenomenon is a well-kept secret. No Palestinian journalist has written about the wave of emigration, which is still increasing," human rights advocate Bassem Eid told Israel's *Haaretz* newspaper. "The thinking is that from a national point of view, the story shouldn't be given publicity . . . . The problem is, that because no one is writing about the phenomenon, no one really knows what the situation is."

Christian citizens of Israel have different concerns. They face discrimination and even disdain as Palestinians, or as Arabs, not as Christians—except among a minority of extreme Jewish nationalists.

In Israel, Christians make up 9 per cent of the country's minority non-Jewish population. Sammy Smooha, a sociology professor at Haifa University, argues that many see themselves as not quite Israeli, or as not Israeli at all. This may not be a problem that compels emigration, but it is an obstacle to Christians' eventual integration into the Israeli state.

For several decades after the 1948 war, the shock of losing land, homes, and livelihood to Israel overwhelmed issues of identification for Arabs. Arabs in Israel were formally under military administration until 1966, and, for decades, land was systematically confiscated from individuals and towns. Christian society was cowed and mostly silent. The government referred to Christians and Muslims as members of the "Arab Sector" and the non-Jewish minorities accepted the unassertive designation of Israeli Arab.

In the year 2000, that changed dramatically. At the outbreak of the Al-Aqsa Intifada, a Palestinian uprising in the West Bank and Gaza against the occupation, Israel's "Arab Sector" protested. Police shot and killed thirteen demonstrators inside Israel. Suddenly, Israeli Arabs shared a common experience with their Palestinian cousins across the Green Line—mistreatment of the kind most had only witnessed on television.

The official Or Commission, set up by the government to investigate the unrest and killings noted that "The feelings of the

Arabs in Israel, whose affiliation with the Palestinians beyond the Green Line aren't just national but social and familial too, were expressed in that famous saying of Abed al-Aziz Zoabi, 'My country is at war with my people.' That doesn't mean the Arab sector as a whole supports all the Palestinians' methods of fighting: the great majority consistently supports the peace process. But at the same time, it utterly identifies with the aspiration to found a Palestinian state, and sees Israeli policy as an obstacle to it."

For Christian Israelis, three modes of self-identification compete with each other. According to Smooha, about 47 per cent of Christians continue to prefer some variation of the old "Israeli Arab" designation.

Increasingly, other Christians refer to themselves as "Palestinian Israeli," or "Palestinian citizen of Israel." Smooha puts this number at almost 29 per cent. Twenty-four per cent identify solely as "Palestinian," without any "Israeli" qualifier. Israeli researchers Ilan Peleg and Dov Waxman observe, "Most Israeli citizens of Arab origin increasingly identify themselves as Palestinian, and most Arab NGOs and political parties in Israel use the label 'Palestinian' to describe the identity of the Arab minority."

Then there's a fourth grouping, a new and smaller one encouraged by Israel's right-wing government and by Christians who say that it's time to move on from the tragedy of 1948, fully identify with the State of Israel and even join the army—where they might have to take up arms against the Palestinians in the West Bank and Gaza Strip. The Israeli government has dusted off an archaic identity to apply to such Christians: Aramaean. It refers to ancient, ethnically diverse peoples who spoke variations of Aramaic, the lingua franca of much of the Holy Land in the time of Christ.

If this stew of contending identities were not enough, fundamentalist Muslims and Jewish extremists have begun to view Christians through a strictly religious lens. The growing Islamist movement in Israel regards Christians as second-class clients in a future Islamic state. Extremist Jews, echoing the radical jihadists, consider Christians polytheists who "worship the Cross" and have no place in the national Jewish homeland.

On June 27, 2015, unknown provocateurs spread leaflets in Jerusalem warning Christians to leave the city for good or face death at the end of the Muslim holy month of Ramadan. "We say to the Christians, unbelievers, you must leave immediately so that you will not be slaughtered like lambs." The leaflets were signed the Islamic State, though no one knew exactly who put them out.

No matter. Church leaders rushed to condemn the statement. Archbishop Hanna said that Palestinian Christians would never leave and that they would stand with Muslim co-nationalists against this threat.

Strong words, for sure, but they only obscured a dual dilemma facing Palestinian Christians in Jerusalem, the West Bank, and Gaza Strip. Creeping radicalization of Palestinian Muslims has become a peril to both Christian lives and Christian allegiance to Palestine.

These fears are relatively new. They are driven in part by reports of radical jihadist persecution of Christians in Syria and Iraq, reinforced by smaller incidents within the Palestinian territories. It is best to visit the homes of Palestinians to hear their concerns, as public airings are rare.

At one such gathering, a Palestinian friend told how a traffic dispute escalated into a mob attack on a Christian-owned souvenir store in Bethlehem. Stone throwers broke windows and employees sat barricaded inside for several hours until police dispersed the crowd. Another described a so-called "extremist hill" in western Bethlehem where Christians fear to venture. A longtime Bethlehem resident told me of pressure on Christian shops to stop serving food during daylight in Ramadan, when Muslims fast.

Bethlehem is not the only focal point of tensions. At least a dozen families have fled from Gaza to Bethlehem following hostile incidents that ranged from verbal harassment of girls in the street for not wearing headscarves to the bombing of the court-yard of a Catholic church last year. In 2006, Muslims attacked churches in Nablus and Tulkarm in protest of remarks by then-Pope Benedict XVI that were deemed insulting to Islam.

The slide to the present state of insecurity has been gradual. The PLO aspired to create a secular state and PLO chief Yasser Arafat was emphatic about the movement's non-sectarian char-acter. In 1995, during a press conference in Gaza, I remember him shouting at a reporter, "This is not Lebanon! This is not Lebanon!" when asked about the possibility of an Islamist–Christian split.

The rise of Hamas challenged the PLO's vision of the future. As set out in its 1988 "covenant," Hamas proclaimed—and contin-ues to insist—that all the land between the Jordan River and the Mediterranean Sea is Islamic holy ground. Its goal was an Islamic State "for Muslim generations until Judgment Day." In an Islamic State, Christians would be subordinate citizens. Peace talks were precluded as efforts by Jews and presumably foreign Christians to beat down Muslims "until they follow their religion." Peace is not possible "except under the wing of Islam."

Hamas' resolve to impose Islamic law over a multicultural, multi-religious Palestine seemed quixotic during the Intifada uprising that began in 1987. Then, the PLO dominated Palestinian politics. Hamas, quietly tolerated by Israel as a rival to the PLO, lay low.

The Intifada was a sustained campaign of overwhelmingly nonviolent civil resistance, a mode of struggle that appealed to Christians. In the town of Beit Sahour, next to Bethlehem, Christian youth eagerly participated in the rebellion: smuggling bread to families during military curfews, spreading leaflets that scheduled strikes and demonstrations, organizing tax strikes, and confronting armed Israeli soldiers with stones. A Christian, Mubarak Awad, promoted a theory of civil disobedience for Palestinians. Israel expelled him to the United States in 1988 for inciting Palestinians to revolt.

But some PLO members already dreaded Hamas' implicitly divisive ideology, thinking it would undermine the secular national struggle (and PLO factions within it). Adnan Barham, then a member of the Popular Front for the Liberation of Palestine, recalls a letter from a PLO delegation in Bethlehem to Khalil al-Wazir—better known as Abu Jihad (the nickname means "Father of Jihad," referring to the name of his eldest son), the PLO official who oversaw the Intifada from exile in Tunis. The letter asked the PLO to declare Hamas a collaborator with Israel. "He never answered," Barham said.

The Intifada led to peace talks and it seemed to many that a resolution to the Israeli–Palestinian conflict was at hand. Israel withdrew from the main West Bank and Gaza cities and Yasser Arafat arrived in the territories to preside over a nascent

Palestinian government. Israelis visited Ramallah and even Nablus, epicenter of the Intifada, for encounters with their old enemies.

As tensions eased, Hamas launched a campaign of suicide bombings inside Israel. Palestinian Christians and Muslims alike reacted negatively and Hamas officials were insulted in the streets, if they dared show their faces. But peace talks stalled, and as Israel constructed more and more settlements in the West Bank, Palestinian frustration grew.

In 2000, the Palestinians launched another Intifada. It followed a visit to the al-Aqsa Mosque complex by the late Ariel Sharon, the right-wing Israeli leader who was soon to become prime minister. He was there to inspect a newly excavated underground mosque. A riot broke out and unrest spread across the West Bank and Gaza.

Arafat called the uprising the al-Aqsa Intifada. It was the first time he had made a religious site the emblem of resistance. Barham noticed the change right away. Bethlehem Christians were told to refer to the struggle as national and Islamic. "We objected," said Barham, "but the order came from on high."

Hamas terror strategy had an impact on Fatah. Worried about being outflanked, Arafat reverted to terrorism. A PLO subunit called the al-Aqsa Martyrs Brigade launched suicide bombings. Christians were comfortable with neither suicides nor a revival of PLO terrorism. They clung to civil disobedience as the best form of resistance, but it was no longer an option: Israel responded right away with unbridled gunfire, and, in any case, since returning from exile, Arafat had sidelined proponents of civil disobedience.

In 2002, the al-Aqsa Martyrs Brigade, seeking refuge from an Israeli assault, took over the Church of the Nativity in Bethlehem and other Christian buildings. Until then, such places had been considered off-limits to combatants. Al-Aqsa Brigade gunmen also commandeered Christian houses in nearby Beit Jala to take meaningless potshots at Jerusalem neighborhoods across the valley. Israel retaliated by smashing through the homes.

Israel crushed the al-Aqsa Intifada and Israeli–Palestinian negotiations continued to stagnate. Misgivings about the way Fatah governed became a major concern among Palestinians. Running on an anti-corruption platform, Hamas won numerous municipal council seats in 2005 elections. "Even Christians voted for Hamas," Barham said. "It was all about corruption."

For many Christians, worrying signs of the meaning of Hamas' political rise soon came into view. In Bethlehem, the elections provided the local Hamas branch with representation in a coalition under a Christian mayor. A Hamas council member, Hassan al-Musalmeh, suggested that jizya, the Islamic poll tax, be imposed on Christians. The proposal never made it to the council.

The following year, Hamas won legislative elections. In 2007, the Islamic group and Fatah engaged in a violent power struggle. Hamas drove Fatah fighters from the Gaza Strip, while Fatah established full control of the West Bank.

Hamas rule in Gaza intensified insecurity for the approximately 3,000 Christians who resided there. On February 15, 2008, arsonists firebombed a library operated by the Young Men's Christian Association and destroyed 10,000 books, police and YMCA officials said. The autumn before, kidnappers killed Rami Ayyad, a Christian bookstore owner, and his bookshop was blown up twice. His mother, foretelling concerns that would intensify later, said, "Before, Israel was the only enemy. Palestinians were together. Now, you don't know who is who."

At the time, Archimandrite Artemios, head priest at St. Porphyrius Greek Orthodox church in Gaza, told me: "Never in Palestinian history did we feel endangered until now. We face the question of whether we are part of this community or not."

Sporadically since then, other incidents have reminded Christians of their vulnerability. Last year, a bomb was placed in a Gaza Roman Catholic convent. A message spray painted on a wall complained about attacks on Muslims in the Central African Republic.

Many Christians have begun to fear that the Islamic State has gained a foothold in the Palestinian territories. "Now, what everyone talks about is Daesh," said Elias Khair, a former PLO police colonel and military trainer.

Khair, who returned with Arafat to the West Bank in 1994, thinks the PLO is ignoring Christian unease at its risk. He complained that Christian officials—mayors and members of the PLO staff—are trotted out for public relations purposes, to display Christian participation in the movement, while Christian worries on the ground are ignored.

Fatah authorities are setting bad examples by marginalizing Christians, he added. "If there are one hundred Christian policemen among the 22,000 in all of Palestine, I'll buy you a bottle of whiskey," he said. "No one wants to speak out about Christian fears. No one wants to say what is on everyone's mind. They only will notice when all the Christians have left."

On any given Saturday at the Maronite church in the ruined village of Biram, in Israel's far north, you can observe the full spectrum of Christian identity in Israel and the source of alienation of many Israeli Christians.

Christians come to Biram to worship and also to protest. They want to return to live in their ancestral village, from which they were expelled in 1948.

The Israeli army had promised residents of both Biram and nearby Ikrit that they could return home. Unlike many Palestinians in the area, the residents did not flee into exile. They waited in the town of Jish. They thought that, as new citizens of Israel, they could trust the authorities.

Permission to return never came.

The citizens of Biram sued in a case that reached the Israeli High Court. In 1951, the court ruled in their favor, but conditional on the government not issuing an "emergency decree" that would forbid reentry. The government quickly issued one.

Then, in 1953, Israel's army provided the decisive answer by shelling the empty houses of Biram while residents looked on from a distance. Ikrit was also leveled.

Land and destruction of towns fundamentally divide the Arab Sector from Jewish Israel. After 1948, hundreds of hamlets—Muslim, Christian, and mixed—were razed and homes were declared abandoned and taken over. Every March 30, Muslims and Christians in Israel gather to commemorate Land Day, which began in 1976 to protest the seizure of almost 5,000 acres of property in Galilee.

The 1948 residents of Biram were not refugees nor had they fought the Zionist armies. They did everything they were told to do and still could not recover their homes. Two farms were founded for demobilized soldiers on the wheat fields of Biram.

For Nagham Ghantous and many other Christians who call Biram home, the standoff reveals her true identity. Whatever her passport says, for Jewish Israel, they are the enemy: Palestinian.

"I'm not really observant, but I'm aware of my Christian inheritance. It was the way we were brought up," Ghantous explained. Her Palestinian consciousness developed by observing the Intifadas, the Arab Spring uprisings, and the regional wars. Inspired by examples of resistance, she is not afraid.

"Biram was destroyed after we were already declared citizens. Its destruction is part of the same project as the conquest of all Palestine, whether Christian or Muslim," she said. Ghantous belongs to al-Awda, a group that supports the return of Palestinian refugees to their homes.

In a 2001 editorial, Israel's *Haaretz* newspaper noted that the state's determined refusal to let Biram residents return stemmed from concern about setting a precedent. If residents of Biram and Ikrit had a right to return, why not those of the many other Arab villages in Israel that had been demolished? And why not the millions of Palestinian refugees?

Since 1984, young people have squatted at Biram in the summertime. They listen to campfire stories about the expulsion, the promises, and the destruction. They cleared a path around the village where the bombed-out stone houses are covered with vines. Last year, officials from the Israel Land Authority and police broke up the camp, confiscated blankets, tents, and mattresses and cut off electricity to a makeshift kitchen.

Even those Christians who identify with Israel want to regain the village. In their view, it is both a test of the rule of law and a reward for their loyalty to the State of Israel. "If we continue to shout about Arab and Palestinian nationalism, nothing will move ahead," activist Shady Halul told an Israeli newspaper. "I believe that if the displaced people of Biram had become integrated, then the demand for their return would be a much stronger one."

Halul calls himself Aramaean and named a son Aram in honor of the new, officially designated nationality. In ancient times, Aramaic speakers populated Syria, Palestine, and parts of present-day Iraq.

Besides teaching Aramaic, Halul heads the Christian Recruitment Forum, a group trying to get Christians to join the Israeli army. He himself served as an officer. Each year, about fifty Christian citizens of Israel join the army, according to a count from Sammy Smooha, the Haifa University researcher.

Halul has said his aim is to detach Christians from the Palestinian conflict and from the Arab world. He feels both identities were thrust on Christians. "We are not part of the Israeli–Arab conflict, but somehow we've been pulled into it," he told the Israeli newspaper *Haaretz*. "We are not Arabs, and we are not Palestinians."

In September 2014, the right-wing Minister of Interior, Gideon Sa'ar, declared Aramaean an official minority. The decision followed a measure proposed by Yariv Levin, a member of Prime Minister Benjamin Netanyahu's Likud Party, to give "separate consideration" to Israel's Christians and "separate them from Muslim Arabs . . . who want to destroy the state from within."

The recruitment drive and the Aramaean identity issue sparked opposition from both Christians and Muslims. In April 2014, a group of young people in Nazareth entered a square dressed as soldiers and set up a mock checkpoint to show how Palestinians are treated. They handed out a pamphlet warning that Israel was trying to turn "the Palestinian national minority into warring sects."

"The reality is that most Christians do not want to serve and will not respond to the call-up," asserted Riah Abu el-Assal, the former Anglican bishop of Jerusalem. Retired Roman Catholic patriarch Michel Sabbah scorned the new Aramaean identity. "It is true that some of us Christians, we spoke Aramaic millennia ago, like the Jews. However history has been ongoing, and has transformed situations and peoples. Today, we are what we are: Palestinians, Arabs, and Christians," he told a conference in early 2015.

No matter how Christians in Israel might view themselves, extremists, be they Jews or Muslims, regard them primarily as heretics. Ghantous noted that, when she speaks with Israeli Islamist activists about citizenship issues, they respond with the assurance that under Islamic law, Christians would be "protected," something she finds disturbing.

Anti-Christian Jewish activity is relatively new. On June 17, 2015, a group of youths from a West Bank settlement of Yitzhar torched a building next to the Church of the Multiplication, where Christians believe Jesus fed a multitude with five loaves of bread and a pair of fish. Yitzhar, which has been patronized by successive Israeli governments, is home to several suspects identified by police as participants in so-called "price tag" attacks on Palestinians. These are carried out throughout the West Bank in response to Palestinian violence and to protest any Israeli government effort to curb settlement building in the West Bank.

The church complex, which sits inside Israel near the Sea of Galilee, suffered damage to its roof and walls, a reception room, and the office of nuns. Dozens of books went up in flames. The arsonists scrawled an excerpt from a Jewish prayer, "Idols will be cast out," on an outer wall.

This was not the only attack by Jewish Israeli extremists on Christian holy places in recent years. Arsonists torched both a Greek Orthodox monastery in West Jerusalem, where they scribbled the word "revenge" on walls, and a monastery in the town of Jabaa. In April 2014, a mob attacked the Multiplication church, damaged crosses, and threw stones at priests and worshippers. In 2013, a fire bomb was thrown at Beit Jimal Monastery near the Israeli town of Beit Shemesh.

Residents of Biram have also experienced anti-Christian vandalism. Five times in the past three years, someone defaced tombs and knocked down crosses on sarcophaguses at the village cemetery. The most recent vandalism took place in April 2015.

In a sectarian environment, how others see you trumps how you see yourself every time. Whether Biram residents identify as Arabs, Palestinians, or Aramaeans, the upshot is the same: they can return to Biram when they die. Even then, may not be left in peace.

8/ WHAT IS TO BE DONE

We are troubled on every side, yet not distressed; we are perplexed, but not in despair; persecuted, but not forsaken; cast down, but not destroyed.
—2 Corinthians 4:8–9

In March 2015, the pope's envoy to the United Nations in Geneva raised the possibility of military intervention to stop and reverse the expulsion of Christians from Iraq and Syria by the Islamic State. In an interview with *Crux*, a Catholic website, Archbishop Silvano Tomasi said Christians in both countries needed help from outside, along with "more coordinated protection, including the use of force to stop the hands of an aggressor."

"We have to stop this kind of genocide. Otherwise we'll be crying out in the future about why we didn't do something, why we allowed such a terrible tragedy to happen," he said.

The words created a sensation—it is not often that a Vatican diplomat advocates warfare. The Vatican quickly tried to roll back Tomasi's words, noting that a statement jointly fashioned by the Vatican, Lebanon and Russia provided to the UN Human Rights Commission, which was, called for no military action. Instead, it asked governments to "reaffirm their commitment to respect the rights of everyone, in particular the right to freedom of religion." Christians face "a serious existential threat from the so-called Islamic State (Daesh) and al-Qaeda, and affiliated terrorist groups, which disrupts the life of all these communities, and creates the risk of complete disappearance for the Christians," the document advised.

The Vatican's conundrum is understandable. Pope Francis is trying to call attention to Christian persecution and get something done about it. But what?

Use of the word "genocide" was an effort to highlight the gravity of the situation. Francis' decision in April 2015 to ascribe the word genocide to the Armenian massacres and displacement of a century ago was aimed at waking up the world to contemporary Christian persecution. In his message, Francis said that "Today too . . . conflicts at times degenerate into unjustifiable violence, stirred up by exploiting ethnic and religious differences. All who are Heads of State and of International Organizations are called to oppose such crimes with a firm sense of duty, without ceding to ambiguity or compromise."

If the pope was hoping for a reaction, he was disappointed.

Global inaction rests firstly on the perception that steps taken to protect Christians would inevitably require further steps to protect all the other minority groups suffering persecution. This is a convenient domino theory used to justify paralysis. The answer to it is simple: because everything can't be done to rescue the downtrodden everywhere, it doesn't mean nothing should be done at all.

The second issue regards the resistance toward treatment of Christians as a special case. It must be made clear that in Iraq, Christians are a special case not because of their religion and supposed affinity with the West. Rather, they are exceptional because they are specifically and systematically persecuted. Such targeted groups should be prioritized even in wartime situations adversely affecting others. To deny asylum to Christians who demonstrably cannot return to their homes is simply discrimination.

First, Iraqi Christians should be offered refuge outside the region, if they wish it. In Iraq, Christian communities no longer can hope to lead a normal life in their homeland. I met refugees and church leaders in Kurdistan who fled Mosul in 2014 and they were as one in insisting that they could never go home. The 12 years since the US invasion of Iraq have been bleak. The present is intolerable and the future holds no hope. They must be offered refuge outside their homeland.

The same can be said of Yazidis, a local Kurdish religious sect under intense attack. Yazidis, not being "People of the Book," have suffered horrific consequences of radical jihad: death, kidnapping, and systematic rape of women.

There are precedents. The United States took in Bosnian refugees and, later, refugees from Kosovo during the 1990s and into the twenty-first century. About 169,000 immigrated. There are also examples from Iraq itself: since 2008, after much official resistance, the United States admitted about 100,000 Iraqis who worked for US occupation officials or who could show grounds they would be persecuted at home.

These numbers refer to permanent refugees, but other models might be also used, such as temporary asylum. Germany hosted 350,000 refugees from Bosnia, and then repatriated all but about 35,000 once the wars in former Yugoslavia subsided. Bosnian refugees are also scattered throughout Western and Central Europe and as far away as Australia.

The number of Christians in Iraq is not, by comparison, impossible to absorb. Iraqi Christians in the country number between 200,000 and 400,000, including those currently in Kurdistan—far less than the 1.4 million or so that lived in Iraq before the 2003 invasion. Even in the anti-immigrant atmosphere that reigns in Europe, the United States, and elsewhere, there is room among several countries for this population.

President Barack Obama, who based his successful bid to be president on his opposition to the Iraq war, could remedy a catastrophic consequence of it by building a new "coalition of the willing" (the name Bush gave to allies in the Iraq war and occupation) to take in refugees. An Iraqi Christian certainly fits the United Nations–endorsed definition of a refugee as someone who is outside his or her homeland and unwilling to return because of "a well-founded fear of being persecuted for reasons of race, religion, nationality, membership of a particular social group, or political opinion."

In 1989, Congress endorsed the Lautenberg Amendment that eased the immigration criteria for Jews and evangelical Christians from the former Soviet Union, Cambodia, Laos, and Vietnam. Under this law, which was later expanded to include religious minorities from Iran, individuals need to provide evidence of possible persecution, rather than proof of its actual occurrence. Today, Iraqi Christians would find it easy to supply evidence of real or conceivable persecution.

"Genocide" is a word that governments are often unwilling to use because it requires action to avert. In the case of Christian persecution in the Holy Land, some formal definitions of "genocide" apply. The 2002 Rome Statute of the International Criminal Court defines genocide as:

> acts committed with intent to destroy, in whole or in part, a national, ethnical, racial or religious group, including: killing members of the group; causing serious bodily or mental harm to members of the group; deliberately

inflicting on the group conditions of life calculated to bring about its physical destruction in whole or in part; imposing measures intended to prevent births within the group; and forcibly transferring children of the group to another group.

Parts of the UN's Convention on the Prevention and Punishment of the Crime of Genocide might also apply. The convention defines genocide as:

action in which armed power organizations treat civilian social groups as enemies and aim to destroy their real or putative social power, by means of killing, violence and coercion against individuals whom they regard as members of the groups.

Perpetrators can be brought to trial at the UN's International Criminal Court.

Islamic State attacks on Christians and other minorities certainly amount to ethnic cleansing. There is no legal definition of ethnic cleansing—meaning the forcible removal of a population—although it has been designated a war crime as one basis for prosecution involving officials from the former Yugoslavia.

Politics, rather than the issue of legal definitions, seems to be the main obstacle to effective relief and protection. The Bush and Obama administrations insisted that the internal Iraqi conflict was not sectarian. This posture excused the US from having to respond to what quickly became a systematic campaign of persecution. Nina Shea, formerly a member of the government's US Commission on International Religious Freedom, said that she approached then–Secretary of State Condoleezza Rice during the Iraq war about protecting Christians. Rice answered that to do that would make the conflict there seem sectarian.

But of course it was. In 2007, when assassinations of priests and the cleansing of neighborhoods in Baghdad and Mosul accelerated, David Satterfield, then the State Department coordinator of Iraq policy, rejected a call for a safe haven in Iraq because it was "against US policy to further sectarianism," Shea said. Christians who approached Paul Bremer, Washington's civilian overseer of the occupation, got the same response: the Americans were in Iraq to defend all Iraqis, not individual groups.

"The problem is that US Iraq policy had many sectarian considerations—except when it came to Christians and other non-Muslims, whom, because they were peaceful, it consistently overlooked," Shea told a Congressional hearing in January 2013.

Europeans are no less reluctant to take meaningful action, though for different reasons. On the political left, there exists an anti-clerical bias that encourages indifference. On the right, the rampant anti-immigration mood hinders concrete manifestations of concern.

Church leaders in the region inadvertently embolden inaction by their reluctance to consider emigration as a solution. They fear the blow to Christian morale in the region. When, in the summer of 2014, France offered asylum to a small number of Iraqis, Greek Orthodox Church leaders in the Levant accused the French of complicity in religious cleansing. They worried it would play into the hands of jihadists who contend Christians have no place in the Holy Land. But the jihadists are not waiting for France or anyone else to finger Christians as targets. The Islamic State and al-Qaeda have made them victims without foreign prodding.

In Syria, the numeric problem—there are two million Syrian Christians—makes an invitation to mass migration into exile less politically realistic than in the Iraqi case. Already, tens of thousands of Syrians, mostly Muslims but some Christians, are storming European shores looking for refuge. Formally taking in such large numbers would be difficult, both logistically and politically. Most European countries are opposed to letting in Syrians at all. The US appears indifferent.

The best that can realistically be done is to provide proper refuge in neighboring countries for refugees of all confessions, whether Christians, Alawites, and Sunnis or others, and press for an end to the conflict. It is also important to register through the United Nations all refugees for possible asylum application, including those, like Christians, who prefer not to live in camps. To repeat: not being able to do everything for everyone does not excuse doing nothing for anyone.

Intuitively, stopping the wars in Iraq and Syria and resolving the Israeli–Palestinian conflict would go a ways toward relieving pressure on minorities.

Unfortunately, no quick fix is in order.

Take Syria and Iraq, where the cast of outside interventionists is large and riven with competing interests. Both conflicts are classic struggles for geopolitical influence. Saudi Arabia, a regional power on one side of the Persian Gulf, supports anti-government rebels in both Syria and Iraq, while Iran, on the other shore, backs the governments of both. In Syria, a reluctant United States is bombing the Islamic State, while an aggressive Russia is bombing all sorts of rebel groups on behalf of Bashar al-Assad, various Persian Gulf states follow Saudi Arabia's lead; and a meddling Turkey backs rebels but is currently more interested in crippling Syrian Kurds than toppling Assad. Meanwhile in Iraq, the United States supports the Shiite government against Sunni rebels funded by Persian Gulf money.

To add fervor to the fighting, religion underwrites geopolitics. In Syria and Iraq, battles have come to be defined as Sunni vs. Shiite contests: Sunni paladin Saudi Arabia takes on Shiite champion Iran.

Framing the struggles in religious terms lets combatants play on ancient sectarian hostilities to intensify passion. For Sunni jihadists, Shiites are enemies because they are "polytheists," and so are Christian, as infidels. They can be killed with impunity.

The Shiite government in Baghdad and the Alawite Bashar al-Assad government in Damascus don't generally justify atrocities against Sunnis in the name of religion, but the gusto with which Shiite militias persecute Sunni communities in Iraq and the penchant of Alawite security force henchmen for killing and torturing Sunnis in Syria indicate an undercurrent of sectarian fervor.

Snapping out of this fury is a distant hope. The Iraq insurgency is in its thirteenth year; the Syrian, in its fifth. Against the backdrop of these grinding stalemates, provision of asylum and safe refuge for targeted victims is the least that must be done.

And then there's Palestine–Israel. The conflict, once seemingly all about land, has become a struggle between strains of Islam and Judaism. Land can be divided; faith cannot. Both religions possess the ethical tools for compromise, but Islamic and Jewish nationalists disavow them. Both these movements are in the ascendancy.

In these circumstances, it is difficult to avoid the conclusion that for Palestinian Christians in the West Bank and Gaza, future prospects are limited to gradual emigration.

Let's say all the wars suddenly ended. Even in that case, conditions in the Middle East that would bring Christians equality and security in the foreseeable future seem unlikely. The failure of Arab Spring probably put off democratic, inclusive reform for at least a generation.

In any event, the concept of full and equal citizenship and, by extension, the end of Christian persecution never much gained traction.

Baathist ideology touched on the idea, albeit by superimposing "Arabness" over the diverse populations of the region (with a nod to the central influence of Islam). Baathist theory expected the many citizens of the region who did not consider themselves ethnically or culturally Arabs at all—Christians among them, but also Kurds and other minorities—to reinvent themselves as such.

The Lebanese formula divided powers among religious sects and supposedly left room for eventual sectarian-blind citizenship. But it never arrived at its ideal destination. Palestinian secular nationalism, meanwhile, is giving way to an Islamic-dominated political identity.

Militant Islamists are drowning the notion of political equality and replacing it with the classic Islamic tradition of the dhimmi, according to which Jews and Christians are free to live under Islam, but only as second-class citizens. Radical jihadists think Christians ought to disappear altogether.

Occasionally, Muslims and Christians have joined together in attempts to secure full citizenship by forging constitutional arrangements that protect equal rights. The efforts have floundered. The failures of Arab Spring were a particular blow.

Following the Tahrir Square protests that overthrew Hosni Mubarak in Egypt, some Egyptians tried to lay out constitutional protections for all. In June 2011, Ali al-Selmy, deputy prime minister of a post-Mubarak interim government, proposed a set of principles to guide the writing of a new constitution. The document was meant to codify the aims of the Tahrir Square uprising. The paper called for the foundation of a "civil democratic state" and declared that "discrimination on basis of gender, race, language, religion, wealth or social status is prohibited."

The language was anathema to Islamists. The Muslim Brotherhood, a key player in Tahrir, threatened street protests. Salafis, whose organized strength surprised many Egyptians, stormed Tahrir to demand the creation of an Islamic state. "The people demand the laws of Allah," they chanted. (Salafis had not taken part in the original Tahrir Square protests.)

The interim government never formally endorsed al-Selmy's guidelines and they disappeared without consequence.

Palestinians might have had a chance to serve as a model, but democratic progress was stymied by the continued conflict with Israel and the authoritarian tendencies of the Palestinian Authority in the West Bank and of Hamas in Gaza.

Secular nationalism among the Palestinians reached its last high point during the first Intifada, the anti-Israeli uprising of the late 1980s and early '90s. Palestinian Christians and Muslims fought the same struggle using the same tactics of civil disobedience.

Subsequent failure to produce a Palestinian state opened the way to a more violent approach. Jihad became the preferred ideological framework among Islamists for the resistance, and Islamic identity became its driving force. Christians found themselves marginalized.

Palestinian politicians, Muslim and Christian alike, nonetheless tried to forge a society based on civil rights, but with very mixed success. In 2003, a new Palestinian constitution came into effect. The document suffered from common contradiction in the region: the coupling of Islam as the dominant ideology with false assertions of equality for all.

Thus, one article designating Islam "the official religion in Palestine" was followed by the injunction that "respect and sanctity of all other heavenly religions shall be maintained." ("Heavenly religions" refers to Christianity and Judaism, effectively ruling out the unlikely rise of, say, Buddhism.)

Another article provided that "The principles of Sharia shall be the main source of legislation," while yet another pledged that "All Palestinians are equal under the law and judiciary without discrimination because of race, sex, color, religion, political views or disability."

The contradictions have never been reconciled. Since 2006, the ruling Fatah faction of the Palestine Liberation Organization has been at war with its main political rival, the Islamist Hamas. In 2007, Fatah and Hamas fought over Gaza and the legislature hasn't met since. Palestinian president Mahmoud Abbas rules the West Bank by fiat, while Hamas reigns in the Gaza Strip. National elections scheduled for 2014 were delayed indefinitely and issues of political equality have been put aside—as they have been across the Holy Land.

+ + + + +

Foreign invasion won't help. Western military interventions have neither promoted tolerance and democracy nor aided liberal Muslim and Christian reformers, who are routinely accused of being Western lackeys. Democratic activists often make a point of distancing themselves from American foreign policy they consider destructive.

The West, if it cares about minorities at all, ought to take a hard look at the dangers of its frequent resort to military force. Historically, Christians suffered inordinately when foreign powers invaded the Holy Land. This was true during the Crusades and true during the long colonial period when European powers carved up the region. Western powers as well as Russia styled themselves the protectors of various Christian communities. Some Christians, viewing foreigners as benefactors, appeared in Muslim eyes to be collaborators.

Michel Sabbah, the retired Roman Catholic patriarch of Jerusalem, described the dilemma of Christians trying to cope with both home grown repression and Western irresponsibility: "Firstly, within each country (in the region), it is an issue of achieving total equality—difficult to attain. Today, with ongoing revolution . . . we are facing the threatening progress of Islamic militias, like ISIS and their like, who have already had an effect on the Christians in Syria and Iraq: massacres and forced emigration.

"Second, the Christian presence in the Middle East is an external question that depends on the West's global political view and planning for the region. Christians do not seem to exist within this planning."

The United States in particular ought to acknowledge its share of responsibility for what happened in Iraq. The war was fought on the basis of a string of falsehoods, among them that Iraq had a nuclear weapons program and Saddam Hussein had something to do with the September 11, 2001, al-Qaeda attacks on New York City and Washington.

Beyond these imaginary justifications, little thought was given to the aftermath. The Bush Administration predicted that a docile society would welcome US occupation. The invasion instead blew the lid off tenuous coexistence among Muslims, Christians, and other minorities, even as enforced by the dictatorial hand of Saddam Hussein.

There is precedent for taking responsibility in the wake of a disastrous war in which the United States played a major role. In 1975, the United States created the Indochinese Refugee Task Force to resettle Indochinese displaced by the Vietnam War. Over 1.4 million were granted entry to the US.

The Bush Administration dismissed warnings provided by the Vatican and other representatives of Christians in Iraq over what would come next. During his visit to Washington in hopes of heading off the war, Vatican envoy Cardinal Pio Laghi handed Bush a letter detailing the dangers: the conflict would cause many casualties, mire the US in the country and result in civil war. The president did not read it during the meeting, according to Vatican accounts. Bush tried to defuse the disagreement by pointing out issues—opposition to abortion and human cloning—on which the White House and Vatican agreed.

Laghi noted that the promotion of life and the family was important, but that the values underlying those policies ought to be applied to the decision to go to war. Bush's deputy vice-chairman of the Joint Chiefs of Staff tried to soothe Laghi and reportedly said, "Your Eminence, don't worry. What we're going to do, we will do quickly and well."

At the end of 2003, during a seminar entitled "God and the Meeting of Civilizations," Laghi recalled telling Bush, "Do you realize what you'll unleash inside Iraq by occupying it?"

Bush, Laghi recalled, "seemed to truly believe in a war of good against evil."

The current wars in Syria and Iraq and political turmoil elsewhere ought to provide plenty of motivation for Christian–Muslim unity on safeguarding religious communities. Christians are under siege, but Muslims suffer extreme violence and repression at the hands of other Muslims.

Radical jihadist intimidation of Sunni Muslims is rampant. Where Islamic law has come into force, restrictions on dress, social habits, and the public role of women have been imposed on all. The tossing of suspected homosexuals off buildings in Syria and the stoning of women accused of adultery are some of the most egregious cases of jihadist rule run amok.

It should therefore be easy for mainstream Sunni communities to see that assaults on Christians are but a prelude to attacks on them. Indeed, fundamentalist terror groups say so explicitly.

As for Iran, reining in the abuses of its Syrian and Iraqi clients would be a recognition of Shiite vulnerability to violence, not only in the Middle East but as far afield as Pakistan and Yemen where Shiites are periodic victims of Sunni Muslim attacks.

Yet, it is difficult to be optimistic. For one thing, traditional interpretations of Islamic doctrine get in the way. Most Muslims in the region are unwilling to surrender the idea that Christians (and Jews) are to be treated as religious sub-species, tolerated but kept underfoot and perpetually vulnerable to abuse. Nor has the violent Sunni–Shiite fever shown signs of abating.

Bigotry has powerful backers. Saudi Arabia, a US ally, has used its immense wealth to spread Wahhabi ideology to Muslims across the globe through television and in mosques. Abd al-Rahman al-Barak, a Saudi cleric, wrote that Saudi Arabia "has the resources to spread Wahhabi message of undying intolerance of peoples who don't accept the one true God, or, as in the case of Christians, those whose conceptions of God are in error."

According to Wahhabi doctrine, Christian sins include permitting men and women to mix in public and encouraging "fornication through the institutions of immorality such as cinemas and dance parlors and singing clubs." Saudi high school textbooks have described Christians ("swine") and Jews ("apes") as the "enemies of believers" who must be fought continuously.

Iran's treatment of minorities at home, where non-Shiites suffer discrimination in housing, jobs, and education, bodes ill for Iraq, where political outreach to minority Sunnis is urgent, and in Syria, where some sort of power-sharing arrangement with the majority Sunni population is needed to end the war.

Against this background of entrenched prejudice, Muslim voices rarely focus on the ideological roots of sectarian conflict. Iyad Ameen Madani, secretary general of the fifty-seven-member state Organization for Islamic Cooperation, denounced the expulsions of Christians from Mosul as having "nothing to do with Islam and its principles that call for justice, kindness, fairness, freedom of faith, and coexistence." Such generic statements are insufficient; they attempt to evade an ideological battle that must be fought head on. Justifications for sectarian persecution, though rooted in literalist interpretations of Islamic doctrine, must be explicitly called out and contested as distortions.

Occasionally an Islamic preacher says out loud what many only think: that fundamentalism, be it in the halls of power in Saudi Arabia and Iran or on the battlefield, furnishes the ideological basis for the killing. According to the Middle East Research Institute website, Brooklyn preacher Tareq Yousef Al-Masri scolded Salafis "who have corrupted the nation of Muhammad, and who have buried our good reputation in the ground." Last year, a Saudi preacher criticized radical Salafis for spreading "the principles of Islam in a twisted manner that makes them incomprehensible or distorted."

Winning the war of ideas is a formidable task. There are nonetheless authoritative Islamic voices, past and present, that can be drawn upon to legitimize the case for tolerance and coexistence. The words of Muslim thinkers like Jamaluddin al-Afghani and Mohammed Abduh, both from the like the nineteenth-century, can be deployed to bolster the case for a rational Islam. Meanwhile key jihadist events and texts, such as the Pact of Omar, can be placed in their historical context to undermine their status as models for the contemporary world.

It is not easy to be an Islamic dissident. The late Egyptian thinker Nasr Hamid Abu Zayd taught students at Cairo University to think beyond the thirteenth-century rigid interpretation of Islamic texts. Cairo University scholars hounded Abu Zayd out of Egypt by trying to force annulment of his marriage, on the grounds that a Muslim woman could not be married to an apostate. The Jamaa Islamiya terror group said he should be killed. He went into exile in the Netherlands with his wife in 1995.

Ahmad Subhi Mansour, another Islamic scholar from Egypt, proposed eradicating brutal teachings from Islam. He was a professor at al-Azhar University but got fired for being, in his words, "an enemy of Islam." He was imprisoned for two months and then in 2002 gained political asylum in the US. In 2011, he protested the Maspero massacre and suggested that construction of churches as well as mosques should be allowed throughout Egypt and that it should be against the law to use any place of worship to promote violence.

Muslim religious and political leaders must build on and assertively promote such opinions not only to preserve Christian life but also save Muslims from chronic violence. It should be done now.

The Sykes–Pico Treaty of World War I, which divided the Holy Land between France and Britain, established the contemporary frontiers of the region. The borders are crumbling and it is worth considering what this means for Christian communities.

The Islamic State has already bitten off parts of Syria and Iraq, established its own "caliphate," and declared an end to the Sykes–Pico era. Iraq itself is currently divided among Shiite, Sunni, and Kurdish regions. Syria is fragmented into areas of government and rebel control. In the event of a total breakup, it is hard to see exactly where either Syrian or Iraqi Christians might find safety.

Among refugees from Mosul and their advocates, there is talk of resurrecting old Assyrian territory in the Nineveh Plain as a "safe haven" and perhaps permanent refuge. The Iraqi government has so far failed to take back any Nineveh territory from the Islamic State, so it is hard to see how secure this haven would be, unless foreigners sent military forces to protect it. Among refugees in Kurdistan I spoke with in 2014, the preferred option was emigration.

In Syria, Christians are spread all over the country and there is no particular geographical area for them to claim as a viable refuge. If the war ends in stalemate, they are fated to remain in areas controlled by the Assad regime, or its successors. As Syria deteriorates further, migration will be the likely solution.

The options of mass exile abroad or the creation of a safe territory near home were unthinkable not long ago. But the unthinkable is happening, and it's time to face the reality of the decline and demise of viable Christian life in the place of Christianity's birth.

In the 1930s, a Lutheran pastor named Martin Niemöller in Germany wrote a poem about the dangers of silence in the face of creeping persecution. He wrote that first the Communists, then the trade unionists, then the disabled, then the Jews suffered Nazi torment. No one said anything. "Then they came for me," the poem concluded. "And there was no one left to speak for me."

The sentiment has become a widely ignored cliché, which is too bad. It is certainly appropriate for the Christian Holy Land. Over time, first the Jews were persecuted; then Christians, then Yazidis. Shiites, many Sunnis, and other Muslims are now endangered.

Will anyone speak up?

SELECTED BIBLIOGRAPHY

Abdul-Hadi, Mahdi. *The Second Arab Awakening.* Jerusalem: Palestinian Academic Society for the Study of International Affairs. 2013.

Aboona, Hirmis. *Assyrians, Kurds and Ottomans: Intercommunal Relations on the Periphery of the Ottoman Empire.* Amherst: Cambria Press. 2008.

Amos, Deborah. *Eclipse of the Sunnis: Power, Exile, and Upheaval in the Middle East.* New York: Public Affairs. 2010.

Asbridge, Thomas. *The Crusades: The War for the Holy Land.* London: Simon & Schuster. 2011.

Bin Talal, Hassan. *Christianity in the Arab World.* London: Continuum Intl Pub Group. 1998.

Cockburn, Patrick. *The Jihadis Return.* London: O/R Books. 2014.

Cook, David. *Understanding Jihad.* Berkeley: University of California Press. 2005.

Herrin, Judith. *Byzantium: The Surprising Life of a Medieval Empire.* New York: Penguin Books. 2008.

Hoyland, Robert G. *In God's Path: The Arab Conquests and the Creation of an Islamic Empire.* Oxford: Oxford University Press. 2015.

Kassis, Rifat Odeh. *Kairos for Palestine.* Palestine: Badayl/Alternatives. 2011.

Lord Kinross. *The Ottoman Centuries: The Rise and Fall of the Turkish Empire.* New York: First Morrow Quill. 1977.

Malaty, Tadros Y. *Introduction to the Coptic Orthodox Church.* Alexandria: St. George's Coptic Orthodox Church. 1993.

Marr, Phebe. *The Modern History of Iraq.* Boulder: The Westview Press. 1985.

Morris, Benny. *1948: Israele e Palestina Tra Guerra e Pace.* Milan: Rizzoli. 2004.

Randal, Jonathan. *The Tragedy of Lebanon: Christian Warlords, Israeli Adventurers, and American Bunglers.* Charlottesville: Just World Books. 2014.

Russell, Gerard. *Heirs to Forgotten Kingdoms: Journeys into the Disappearing Religions of the Middle East.* London: Simon & Schuster. 2014.

Sharpe, Samuel. *The History of Egypt Under the Romans.* Edward Moxon. 1842.

Smith, George Adam. *The Historical Geography of the Holy Land.* London: The Fontana Library Theology and Philosophy. 1966.

Tayah, Wadih Peter. *The Maronites.* Miami: Bet Moroon. 1987.

Ulph, Stephen and Sookhdeo, Patrick. *Reforming Islam: Progressive Voices From the Arab Muslim World.* McLean: Almuslih Publications. 2014.

OR Books

PUBLISHING THE POLITICS OF THE MIDDLE EAST